More Praise for *Building on the Promise of Diversity*

"Dr. Thomas, truly the leading thinker in diversity management, now offers us his latest evolution—the craft of Strategic Diversity Management. The argument Dr. Thomas makes for SDM is both compelling and practical. And while he focuses on the 'diversity experiment' in the United States, SDM and the ideas in this book apply to everyone around the world."

—Julie O'Mara, O'Mara and Associates, consultant and author, former national President of The American Society for Training and Development

"Roosevelt Thomas has written a thoughtful and scholarly book. While other thinkers in this field may arrive at different conclusions, we are all immeasurably indebted to him for providing a broader platform to think pioneering thoughts and take groundbreaking actions in helping resolve some of America's most important and urgent issues."

—Price M. Cobbs, M.D., author of *My American Life: From Rage to Entitlement* and co-author of *Cracking the Corporate Code*

"Roosevelt Thomas challenges all members of our pluralistic societies to step forward, individually and collectively, to learn to manage our similarities and differences, and to accept their related tensions. The craft he presents us is an ongoing learning experience, a universal model, and goes way beyond the traditional ones offered until now. If first applied in our schools, it would equip future generations with the tools and skills needed to define and understand common goals and requirements upon which to base quality decision-making processes."

—Monique Seefried, Ph.D., President, Council of Foundation, International Baccalaureate Organization

"In *Building on the Promise of Diversity*, Dr. Roosevelt Thomas has continued to spark and refresh the dialogue on diversity. The book asks us to consider that the current ideology on diversity is heading toward complacency, and it provides an important new framework for organizations that are embarking on or renewing their diversity efforts."

—Ana Duarte McCarthy, Director, Global Workforce Diversity, Citigroup

"Roosevelt Thomas teaches through stories, clarifies with definitions, and challenges with passion. He shares a personal account of how his views have changed over the years, chronicles the history of inclusion/exclusion, civil rights, and affirmative action in the United States from the perspective of diversity management, and gives us the tools we need to move from our current state of being 'stuck' to implementation of Strategic Diversity Management concepts. A must read for any leader who wants to understand how to make quality decisions in the midst of differences, similarities, and tension."

    —Mary-Frances Winters, President and CEO, The Winters Group, Inc.,
       and author of *Inclusion Starts with I* and *Only Wet Babies Like Change*

"Building on the Promise of Diversity is powerful and fresh, the result of a compelling personal and professional voyage in the field. Roosevelt Thomas reminds us why understanding and leveraging diversity remains the key to success in a global economy, and shows us clear strategies for developing the craft and skills of diversity management."

    —Sally Helgesen, author, *The Female Advantage* and *The Web of*
      Inclusion

"This book is a defining piece aimed at elevating readers' thoughts on diversity. It is a blueprint of how great cultural/societal changes can occur not only in the workplace but in society. This is a must read for those who are still locked in the old concept of what diversity means."

    —Paul Campbell, VP of Human Resources/Labor Community
      Relations & Diversity, Polo Ralph Lauren

"It's not common to find so much in one book, but this book is uncommon. It's rare because it makes you think and feel as well as inspires you to take action. This is a wonderful book on a subject that is a challenge for nearly everyone. Refreshing, interesting, and helpful."

    —Rick Culley, President, Institute for Executive Development

"Dr. Thomas is one of our nation's foremost experts on diversity and the management of diversity. This book is the result of his twenty years of thinking, writing, lecturing, and leadership, and is the capstone to his thought. The book is a must read for all of those in leadership who want to step up and make a difference as they work with the complexities of diversity. It touches every area in which we live, which makes it a most compelling subject indeed."

    —George H. Tooze, President, Ministers and Missionaries Benefit Board

"This is the new thinking on diversity that must be discussed and debated in today's world. Dr. Thomas's work continues to be insightful, compelling, and practical."

    —Marcia Williams, Vice President, Diversity, Albertson's

"With a clear, vigorous voice, Dr. Thomas takes us on a journey of where we have been, our current state, and where we must go with diversity. The challenge he presents leaves no one out. Whether it is on a personal, organizational, or societal level, the critical question is: Are we able to make *quality* decisions in the mist of diversity with its accompanying tension and complexity? Readers are provided with tools and processes to develop the 'craft' of using the Strategic Diversity Management framework as the means to get them there."

—Kay Iwata, K. Iwata Associates, Inc.

"Dr. Thomas's process gives organization leaders a new analytic method for understanding and acting on the natural tensions that arise when any group works together. The process can help to focus both managers and team members on their common work goals and to understand the different perspectives and assumptions that each team member brings to the work. Very importantly, it provides a way for the entire team to suggest innovations and to shape a new organizational culture and action plan that makes best use of the talents and abilities at hand to achieve success."

—Joanne Scanlan, Senior Vice President, Professional Development, Council on Foundations

"This book will take you on a journey with the diversity guru Dr. Roosevelt Thomas, from his early thinking on the subject to his best work, *Building on the Promise of Diversity*. The book belongs in your tool kit if you want to examine the craftsmanship required for Strategic Diversity Management."

—Edward W. Bullock, Vice President of Diversity, L'Oreal, USA

"Dr. Thomas challenges some of the very sacred core, traditionally held concepts that America should be attempting to understand and implement when it comes to appreciating diversity initiatives in the home, workplace, and community. He succinctly outlines how managing diversity, in its broadest definition, can promote changed behavior. This book can be a powerful, thought-provoking catalyst to generate an effectively meaningful diversity management program."

—Gerald L. Durley, Pastor, Providence Missionary Baptist Church

"Dr. Thomas takes the understanding of diversity to a new level. Through Strategic Diversity Management, organizations can achieve breakthrough performance making quality decisions to accomplish their goals. This book is a great primer for profit and nonprofit organizations alike."

—Tim Toppen, President, Engineered Products, The Goodyear Tire & Rubber Co.

"Roosevelt Thomas has been tirelessly committed to seeking the next ways to keep the promise of diversity alive and moving forward. This is no mean feat, as the topic of diversity is both profound and subtly elusive. The Strategic Diversity Management framework presented in his latest work is loaded with usable wisdom. This book serves as a powerful guide for all readers, whatever their diversity challenges, to help deepen commitment and sharpen skills in diversity leadership."

 —Christopher Cappy, President, Pilot Consulting Corporation

"This book provides a refreshing 'breath of resuscitation' for the dialogue around Strategic Diversity Management. The framework outlined is critical to moving the practice of diversity management past its current state of being 'stuck.' It engages the reader in a holistic view of the personal, organizational, and community imperatives for making quality decisions in the midst of diversity tensions that impact both our personal and professional lives. A must read for all diversity practitioners, from the novice to the most seasoned vets."

 —David L. Casey, VP, Diversity & Workplace Culture, WellPoint, Inc.

"Roosevelt Thomas's approach to managing diversity is both sensible and sustainable. Here is a blueprint that gets us past the failures of single-minded fixation on race or gender and shifts the focus to how to manage the true diversity mixtures that we all know are present. This approach embraces the inevitable tensions that surface around issues of diversity as a sign of health to be managed rather than as a problem to be hidden by keeping them suppressed below the surface."

 —David B. Hawley, Headmaster, Atlanta International School

"Roosevelt's latest book introduces the concept of Strategic Diversity Management as a universal and practical venue for quality decision-making with individuals, organizations, and communities."

 —Thomas Phillips, former Quaker Oats executive; co-recipient of 2005
  Lifetime Achievement Award in Black Philanthropy

"Once again Dr. Roosevelt Thomas has provided the most comprehensive thesis on diversity available today. *Building on the Promise of Diversity* delivers a how-to guide to improve both individual and organizational effectiveness. The craft of Strategic Diversity Management applied to all levels of decision-making can deliver that competitive advantage that all individuals and organizations are looking for."

 —John Weaver, VP of Human Resources, Ametek Corporation

BUILDING ON THE PROMISE OF DIVERSITY

HOW WE CAN MOVE TO THE NEXT LEVEL IN OUR WORKPLACES, OUR COMMUNITIES, AND OUR SOCIETY

R. Roosevelt Thomas, Jr.

American Management Association

New York • Atlanta • Brussels • Chicago • Mexico City • San Francisco
Shanghai • Tokyo • Toronto • Washington, D.C.

Strategic Diversity Management (SDM) and the Strategic Diversity
Management Process are trademarks of R. Thomas & Associates, Inc.

Library of Congress Cataloging-in-Publication Data

Thomas, R. Roosevelt.
        Building on the promise of diversity : how we can move to the next level in
    our workplaces, our communities, and our society / R. Roosevelt Thomas, Jr.
            p. cm.
        Includes bibliographical references and index.
        ISBN 0-8144-0862-1
        1. Diversity in the workplace—United States—Management.   2. Organizational
    change—United States—Management.   3. Minorities—Employment—United
    States.   4. Strategic planning—United States.   5. Social change—United States.
    I. Title.

    HF5549.5.M5T463   2006
    658.3' 008—dc22   2005018206

Printing number

10   9   8   7   6   5   4   3   2   1

To my wife, Ruby,
and our sons and daughter—
Walter, April, and Jarred.

CONTENTS

P R E F A C E

DIVERSITY, and the tensions that inevitably accompany it, have existed at our country's core from the beginning. Diversity considerations provoked the Revolutionary War, influenced the nature and content of the United States Constitution, sparked the Civil War, generated race riots in the 1960s, and produced today's "cultural wars."

Clearly, diversity is as American as apple pie, and just as widespread. Equally clearly, it can be a source either of endless challenges and dissension, or of ongoing opportunities. We determine which by the effectiveness with which we address diversity. The more proficient our nation and its organizations and communities become in making quality decisions in the midst of diversity, the better off we will be as a country. Two critical terms in the preceding sentence need explanation, since I will use them in a particular way throughout this book:

- *Diversity* refers to the differences, similarities, and related tensions that exist in any mixture. Note especially that the term includes differences *and* similarities. Diversity is not limited to issues of race and gender, nor is it confined to the workforce.

- *Quality decisions* are decisions that are aligned with the goals of a larger entity—the organization, community, or society—and the individuals within it.

This book is for leaders of all kinds who are frustrated with their own, their organization's, or their country's inability to cope with diversity. They want to see the promise of diversity fulfilled.

Some of these leaders hold formal leadership positions. Others have earned the title of leader because they are willing to push the state of the art with diversity—to move to the next level.

Both types of leaders grapple with differences and similarities of all kinds, and the resulting tensions and frustration that they experience are very real.

However, they differ in two important respects. Some leaders recognize that they are dealing with diversity; others do not. Some openly call for efforts to move to a higher level, even when it is unfashionable to do so. Others strive more quietly to work through and beyond their diversity challenges.

These leaders may come from business and include:

- Corporate managers struggling with workforce diversity issues

- Executives working to overcome barriers to integrate the entities of a merger or an acquisition

- Corporate executives facing the challenges of globalism

Other diversity leaders come from society at large and may include:

- Citizens trying to make sense of persistent, divisive "cultural wars"

- Citizens concerned about the country's increasing political divisiveness

- Community officials trying to get their arms around an increasingly multicultural group of constituents

- Homemakers tirelessly assuming multiple roles

- University presidents trying to satisfy the widely divergent agendas and expectations of various faculty members

■ Ministers coping with racial and ethnic tensions in their pluralistic congregations

■ Weary social justice advocates pursuing the elusive objectives of their movements

I wrote this book to stimulate diversity leaders of all kinds to engage in pioneering thinking and groundbreaking action. Both are essential. I am convinced that getting better at the status quo will not take us where we need to be. Progress to the next level will require new thinking and bold, nontraditional actions that confront paradigms and tactics that are no longer sufficient.

Toward that end, I work with seven broad themes in this book:

1. Contrary to popular thought, diversity is not solely—or even primarily—about improving racial and ethnic relations in the midst of pluralism. Diversity refers to *any* set of differences and similarities in *any* setting.

2. Diversity management (i.e., making quality decisions in the midst of diversity) is not the same as diversity itself. Unlike diversity, diversity management has received little attention to date.

3. Diversity management has the potential to enhance the quality of decision making in *any* setting; it is not limited to the traditional focus on race and gender in the workplace.

4. Diversity management is an essential life capability. Throughout our lives, all of us—individually and collectively—are called upon to make all kinds of quality decisions while beset by differences, similarities, and related tensions. How well we make these decisions can be pivotal for our lives.

5. Part 3 of this book details Strategic Diversity Management (SDM)™, a craft that I have evolved over the past twenty years for achieving effective diversity management. Like all crafts, it consists of concepts, fundamentals, mind-set, skills, and tools; and like all crafts, its mastery demands practice.

6. The Strategic Diversity Management Process (SDMP)™ is a key tool of the craft. This process integrates the concepts and fundamentals into a five-step framework that can facilitate quality decision making amid diversity. Practice with this tool can lead to mastery of the craft.

7. Strategic Diversity Management can be used universally with *any* diversity mixture, and it can serve as the bridge to greater effectiveness with diversity wherever you find it.

My hope is that you will embrace a leadership role—that you will not settle for the status quo with diversity, but will instead be willing to think pioneering thoughts *and* take groundbreaking actions. My belief is that this book can provide you with the understanding and skills to allow you to do both.

Toward that end, I have included as an appendix an instrument, Mastering the Basics: A Critical Step Toward Diversity Maturity—Your Personal Coach, that you can use to facilitate your first pioneering steps toward greater effectiveness with diversity management.

ACKNOWLEDGMENTS

THE TIMING OF THIS BOOK PROJECT is around a personal and professional milestone: the twentieth anniversary of my founding of the American Institute for Managing Diversity (AIMD), a nonprofit think tank devoted to advancing the field of diversity. As you might imagine, this celebration sparks a range of emotions and a flood of appreciative thoughts of how I have been helped with this book and others.

First, I thank my wife and family for their tolerance of my passion for diversity. Without their support, this book and other efforts over the twenty-year period would have been much more difficult.

I also am appreciative to former Morehouse College presidents Dr. Hugh M. Gloster and Dr. Leroy Keith for their support of AIMD during its earlier years. Having been housed initially at Morehouse facilitated the Institute's launching.

Intellectually, I am indebted to Harvard Business School professors Paul R. Lawrence and Jay W. Lorsch, whose work on the differentiation and integration of functions in organizations provided the jumping-off point for my thinking around diversity and diversity management. The influence of their groundbreaking research can be seen readily in my writings.

Melanie Harrington, Executive Director of AIMD, read the chapter on affirmative action. Her feedback was very helpful as I sought to be clear and accurate regarding affirmative action.

Dr. Walter E. Fluker, Executive Director of Morehouse College's

Leadership Center, and Reverend Randy Johnson, a civil rights activist and assistant minister of Friendship Baptist Church in Atlanta, read the chapter on the Civil Rights Movement. Both provided useful insights on the Movement and Dr. Martin Luther King, Jr.

In addition, Marcia Williams of Albertson's read the complete manuscript and offered comments from her perspective as a diversity practitioner. Her comments contained helpful affirmations, questions, and cautions.

I also acknowledge with gratitude the staff of Roosevelt Thomas Consulting & Training (RTCT) for their support in refining the Strategic Diversity Management Craft (SDMC) through consulting applications in a number of settings. Each application has enabled us to learn more about SDMC and to enhance the framework's potential. Their pioneering, innovative efforts have been most encouraging.

I appreciate the leaders and associates of the corporations and other organizations that have allowed me to learn about diversity and diversity management with them. These findings have provided the foundation on which this book and previous ones have been based.

I am particularly indebted to the fellows of Diversity Leadership Academy of Atlanta and the Diversity Leadership Academy of Greater Indianapolis for the opportunity to facilitate their exploration of the craft of SDM. The participants' enthusiasm for learning about new perspectives generated invaluable dialogue that further refined my thinking about the craft of SDM.

Torri Griffin, Anthony Griffin, Elizabeth Holmes, Kathy Lee, David Rupp, and Marjorie Woodruff worked on the different versions of the coaching instrument Mastering the Basics. Their efforts facilitated the design and content of the instrument.

For the fourth time, I have enjoyed the benefits of working with Adrienne Hickey, AMACOM senior acquisitions and planning editor. She provided insightful guidance throughout the process, and I very much appreciate her assistance.

Also, once again, Marjorie Woodruff and Maggie Stuckey provided editorial assistance as I prepared the manuscript for submission. I thank them for their professionalism and commitment to the project.

I thank Becky Hess for word processing the manuscript. Her cooperative spirit greatly facilitated the project.

Finally, but not least, I appreciate the support of TEC (The Executive Committee) Group 242, chaired by Manola Robison. Their consistent and friendly inquiries about the book's progress helped me to stay close to my various target dates.

While I express gratitude for the direct and indirect contributions that have been given, I fully accept responsibility for the book.

INTRODUCTION

CHAPTER

DIVERSITY

IN SEARCH OF THE NEXT LEVEL

ACROSS AMERICA these days, leaders of all types of organizations are voicing disillusionment about the current state of diversity. It is an enormous topic, with enormous consequences.

While typically we tend to think of diversity as being a concern of the business world, this state of anxiety is not limited to corporate CEOs. Leaders of other organizations—religious, educational, governmental, and social action groups—express the same misgivings.

"I'm concerned that we have plateaued" is a common sentiment. "Where do we go from here?" they ask. "We've got to raise diversity a notch if it's to meet today's challenges." Even though they articulate their concerns in different ways, intuitively these leaders are all searching for the same thing—a way to move to the next level.

Talking with them brings to mind the refrain from an old Peggy Lee hit. "Is that all there is," she sings in a world-weary voice as great expectations go unfulfilled. Indeed, weary is how many of us feel. What happened, they wonder, to the original promise? They yearn for a lasting solution to the equal-representation conundrum so that they can focus on other areas.

Evidence of both weariness and yearning abound. Corporate leaders gear up for the latest diversity effort, imploring their organizations to "do something different, so we don't have to do it again." Leaders in all sectors debate the "right wordings," as if semantics were the bridge to the next level. Diversity? Inclusion? Multiculturalism? Cultural competency? Attendance at "best practices" conferences is brisk as organizations search for the panacea that will catapult them to the next diversity level. Community leaders fret about potential Balkanization.

Underlying all of this sentiment is an unspoken fear: "What if there is no next level? What if this is as good as it gets?" I don't think it is. But an old folk saying comes to mind: Nothing changes if nothing changes. If we're unwilling to change what has gone wrong, this may indeed be as good as it gets.

THE POLITICIZING OF DIVERSITY

Currently, most organizational leaders, along with the broader society in the United States, subscribe to a politicized definition of diversity—namely, that it is a code word for affirmative action. In that coded sense, diversity means fostering the recruitment, promotion, and retention of members of "protected classes." The hope is that using the term *diversity* will avoid the stigma that has traditionally been attached to affirmative action.

"I believe in diversity."

"I respect diversity."

"We promote diversity."

"Diversity is good for business."

Statements such as these, so familiar in the business world, are tip-offs to this approach. They suggest that diversity is something that must be created or sanctioned. Yet diversity, per se, disentangled from its politicized definition, need not be approved of or promoted. It already exists. It simply is.

Whenever I describe myself as active in the diversity arena, I inevitably have to explain that diversity is not synonymous with affirmative action and equal opportunity. And yet, wherever I turn, I see evidence of the tightness of the affirmative action/diversity knot. When I make presentations based on my understanding of diversity, someone always comes up afterward and says, "That was not what I expected." Many people come prepared to hear me discuss "diversity" as a euphemism for affirmative action.

A content analysis of "best diversity practices" supports my personal experience. Factors related to "the numbers" or "the representation of minorities and women" are often cited as the rationale for diversity efforts. In *Diversity Inc.*'s 2004 listing of the qualities of the Top 50 Companies for Diversity, for example, four of the six most frequently mentioned factors concerned the representation of minorities and women (see Figure 1-1). In *Fortune* magazine's 50 Best Companies for Minorities, the five most frequently cited rationales also deal with representation (see Figure 1-2).

Implications

I believe that the predominant use of the term *diversity* as a euphemism for affirmative action has significant negative consequences. Affirmative action is the subject of considerable controversy and debate. To equate the terms is to tarnish diversity's credibility with those who discredit affirmative action.

It is also to assume that the word *diversity* has no substance of its own. This assumption is doubly harmful. It hamstrings our ability even to identify diversity in its broadest sense—as something that exists beyond the workplace—and to develop appropriate processes for its management; it also inhibits our ability to recognize that such identification and processes are needed. This is not a question of altruism, but rather business necessity. Corporate leaders in particular would do well to turn their attention to identifying and addressing diversity outside of the workforce (more about this subject in Chapters 7 and 8), simply because it can produce considerable financial rewards.

Perhaps most destructive, however, is that politicizing any issue turns it into a power struggle. One side must win; the other must lose. By politicizing diversity, we have hindered greatly our ability to work creatively and flexibly to develop techniques that complement the traditional affirmative action framework. Those who discredit affirmative action feel validated; those who want to promote it feel frustrated.

FIGURE 1-1
Diversity Inc.'s qualities of the Top 50 Companies for Diversity.*

Item	Frequency
Recruitment and retention	22
Constant attention to diversity numbers/metric measures	17
Diversity education, training, and programs	16
Community involvement/philanthropy	16
Supplier diversity	15
Women hired and promoted to higher-level positions	14
Involvement, support, and leadership from CEO/president	10
Rewards, bonuses, or monetary incentives for diversity	8
Mentoring programs	8
Multicultural marketing	7
People of color hired and promoted to higher-level positions	6
Support from managers and senior executives	5
Partnerships with outside organizations	5
Communication between upper-level/lower-level/community/ vendors/consumers	4
Emphasis on the individual	3
Hiring of interns of color	2
Hiring of people with disabilities	1
Total	159

SOURCE: This figure was developed from data presented in "Top 50 Companies for Diversity," *Diversity, Inc.* (June–July 2004), pp. 46–110.
*Frequency refers to the number of times the item was cited as rationale for including a corporation on the list.

The Difficulty of Change

Even people who have grown weary of the endless diversity cycle and wish to approach diversity differently find that it is not easy to do so, given the entrenchment of the code-word definition.

One reason this definition is so entrenched is that diversity is

FIGURE 1-2
Fortune magazine's qualities of the 50 Best Companies for Minorities.

Item	Frequency
Minorities hired or promoted to high-level positions	29
Retention and recruitment	18
Minorities included among the best-paid employees	13
Minorities included on the board of directors	12
Large amount of the workforce (25 percent or more) is minority	12
Diversity, education, training, and programs	10
Support, leadership, involvement, and accountability from managers and senior executives	9
Minority president/CEO/COO/VP	7
Minority suppliers/vendors	5
Involvement, support, and leadership from CEO/president	5
Mentoring/management tracking/succession programs	5
Diversity task force/panels/committees	5
Rewards, bonuses, or monetary incentives for diversity	4
Community involvement/philanthropy	4
Hiring of interns of color	4
Partnerships with outside organizations	3
Constant attention to diversity numbers/metric measures	1
Focus on the individual	1
Total	147

Source: This figure was developed from data presented in "50 Best Companies for Minorities," *Fortune* (June 28, 2004), pp. 136–146.

widely seen as a legacy of the Civil Rights Movement. Arguing to free "diversity" from its current politicized definition can be seen as arguing to abandon that movement, something few want to see. As a result, the politicized definition will likely continue until the perceived incentive for definitional change outweighs the disincentive.

There are, however, substantial incentives for *complementing* the prevailing definition. I believe that as people think more deeply about diversity, they will become aware of its roots independent of affirmative action and the Civil Rights Movement. They will explore the potential of universal definitions to foster quality decision making. Then they will look for ways to develop complementary relationships between traditional and universal definitions of diversity. This book is an effort to encourage that to happen.

REQUIREMENTS FOR MOVING TO THE NEXT LEVEL

Three things seem critical to defining and attaining the next level of diversity effectiveness:

1. Serious and deep thinking about diversity approaches

2. Developing approaches that can be used by leaders and individual contributors alike

3. Developing approaches that can be applied to both organizational (micro) and societal (macro) diversity issues

Serious Thinking

Collective and individual thought must be given to core questions about our approach to diversity issues. Helpful questions include the following:

- What events or ideas are the source of my (our) diversity-related thinking?

- What fundamental concepts (i.e., definitions), principles, and frameworks undergird my (our) thinking?

- How did my (our) thinking evolve to this point?

It is important to explore your thinking over time because, like maps, even good approaches can become outdated. During my twenty-plus years of addressing diversity, my understanding of it has matured. My thinking has evolved beyond frameworks that once proved extremely helpful but later became inadequate. (This personal odyssey, offered to you as an example, is described in Chapter 6.) Deep, serious thought along these lines will help you to spot needed revisions.

Effective Diversity Approaches

The value of any approach is how fully it allows us to address related issues. So the core question for a given diversity approach becomes: Do the concepts, principles, and tools help me to understand and navigate the dynamics of the diversity I encounter? If they do, the approach is valuable; if not, there is need for change.

One change is needed in nearly all organizations: We must develop approaches that can be used by everyone. Current practices focus on equipping leaders and managers to address diversity and ignore individual contributors. Where rank-and-file employees do engage in diversity "programs," it is assumed that buy-in by management is what really matters. In practice, it sometimes appears that responsibility for diversity effectiveness always rests with someone else. Typically, I hear three refrains:

Executives say: "We get it at the highest levels; middle management is the problem."

Managers say: "Management gets it. Our challenge is the employee ranks."

Employees say: "This won't work without senior management leadership."

Who doesn't get it may be a moot point. Success with diversity requires effectiveness from *all* people in the organization. Unfortunately, for large and small entities, working diversity issues at all levels can be a daunting challenge. In one mammoth enterprise, a senior executive asked, "Do you realize how large we are? Do you know how difficult it is to bring about change?"

I do recognize the magnitude of the challenge, and I certainly know how hard it is to bring about change. But diversity effectiveness must exist at all organizational levels, and developing approaches that work for everyone has become critical.

Finally, we must simultaneously address diversity issues at both the micro level (organizations) and macro level (society). Most forums tend to address one or the other. Yet micro and macro issues provide context for each other; the effectiveness of one affects the success of the other.

Leaders in all fields recognize this fact. Corporate executives complain, "How can I deal with organizational diversity as you prescribe when society lags far behind us?" Meanwhile, leaders of organizations that advocate for societal change ponder how to get corporations to do better with diversity issues. Indeed, this concern was the genesis for the Civil Rights Act and affirmative action. Societal observers such as John W. Gardner have noted the need to address diversity in communities to reverse the trend of growing fragmentalization.[1]

If we are to achieve the next level of diversity effectiveness, we must find approaches that can be used readily with *both* micro and macro issues, because they are interdependent. Such approaches would play a major role in securing across-the-board progress and addressing the challenges of increased community diversity.

SHOULD LEADERS CARE?

At this point you may be thinking, "I understand what you are saying about going to the next level, but I don't feel any urgency. Really, is diversity still a challenge? Is there really a need for another book on diversity?"

This perspective reflects a belief that organizations have put diversity to bed. Leaders who hold this view typically believe the following about their situations:

■   We have made significant progress in moving toward proportionate racial and ethnic representation in our workforce. Our weaknesses can be traced to an inadequate supply of qualified minorities, a circumstance that we are seeking to remedy through scholarships and internships. Indeed, our corporation and others have won awards for our efforts with representation.

■   We have stamped out any symptoms that suggest discrimination exists. Without a doubt, we are now discrimination free.

■   Through awareness and respect, we have achieved and maintained harmony among the different racial and ethnic subcultures.

■   Nobody is jumping up and down claiming we have diversity problems. And even if problems should occur, we know how to minimize the damage.

These leaders logically wonder, "Why should we disturb the status quo? Why can't we pronounce our diversity efforts a success and move to the next challenge? Do we really need any more explorations of diversity?"

My answer is a resolute "Yes, you do." Six reasons come to mind:

1.   Rank-and-file participants in your organization do not share your rosy view about progress with diversity. They often ask me, "Roosevelt, has there been *any* progress over the past twenty years?" When I detail what I consider to be accomplishments, their responses are along the line of, "Okay, if you say so—but I'm not convinced."

2.   Just below the "harmonious" surface is a simmering uneasiness. Many employees feel a lack of connectedness, cohesiveness, and a sense of belonging. Even as they are moving up the organizational ladder, the rank and file experience a lack of integration.

3.   Most leaders assume that achieving harmony is the goal, and they stop there. But even when there is racial and ethnic harmony, and in a setting certifiably free of racism, sexism, and other "isms," conditions generating racial and ethnic tension can thrive. The very presence of multiple races and ethnicities can give rise to differences and related complexities.

4.   If they have not prepared for these complexities, leaders can experience difficulty making quality decisions.

5. If we move beyond the politicized definition of diversity as code for affirmative action and instead accept it as a set of differences and similarities along any dimension, it readily becomes clear that organizations face enormous, ongoing diversity issues. Lingering acquisition/merger concerns; interrelationships between functions and departments; relationships with consumers or clients; concerns about innovation, products, and services; relationships with the larger community—any or all of these, and an infinite number of other possibilities, create a challenge to making quality decisions. Interestingly, leaders know this at a gut level. When I am asked what I do for a living, how I respond determines the reaction I receive. If I say, "I am a diversity consultant," I get one of those "Are people still doing that?" looks. But if I say, "I help people make quality decisions in situations where there are differences, similarities, and related tensions," I get a warm, interested response. "That sounds interesting," they say. "We have some of those challenges." The challenges they're talking about go beyond race and gender and beyond the politicized definition of diversity.

6. Finally, even if organizations have their act together, communities do not. Community leaders and commentators openly worry about splintering.[2] Since business organizations do not operate in a vacuum, their leaders must address the influence that community issues have on their efforts to manage diversity effectively.

In sum, organizational leaders who boast that they have completed their diversity agenda are essentially in denial. I guarantee you that unrecognized or unacknowledged diversity issues will compromise your organization's efforts in pursuit of its mission, vision, and strategy, if they are not already doing so. Leaders who persist with a head-in-the-sand approach do so at their peril.

DIVERSITY MANAGEMENT: THE CRAFT

As you perhaps have surmised by now, this book is not so much about diversity per se, but rather more about managing differences and similarities through a formalized process of diversity management. Fostering mastery of the craft of diversity management is a central aspect of this book.

You may be surprised that I speak of "craft" in this context. Set aside any visions you may have of embroidered denim or scented potholders. Think instead of the exquisite craftsmanship of a master cabinetmaker, or the artistry behind stained glass windows in a cathedral. Imagine the years and years of work devoted to perfecting these crafts to their highest level.

In their book *The Communication Catalyst,* Mickey Connolly and Richard Rianoshek provide a view of "craft" that is compatible with my thinking about diversity management. They define craft as "the collected concepts and skills that are fundamental to success in a particular area of achievement." It is, in their view, distinct from talent, which they consider the "special natural ability with which a person is blessed."[3]

Some people have a natural talent for making quality decisions in the midst of diversity. In *Building a House for Diversity,* I described two such leaders: Phil Jackson, former coach of the Chicago Bulls and the Los Angeles Lakers, and "Bill Smith," a general manager in a large corporation.[4] More recently, during a 2004 presentation made at the Diversity Leadership Academy of Greater Indianapolis, I learned of another case of an elementary school principal with extraordinary accomplishments in a low-income, multiracial, multiethnic community. Most of us, however, do not have a natural bent for the craft of diversity management. We have to learn how to master it.

When I refer to the "craft of diversity management," I have in mind dual elements: art and skill. For the naturally talented, the craft is mostly art. Often, they can't easily articulate why and how they are so effective with diversity management. For others—the vast majority, I suspect—the craft is largely learned skills. Sometimes, people use acquired skills so thoroughly and for so long that they eventually cultivate a natural inclination, so the skills ultimately become art.

How do you master a craft? Connolly and Rianoshek say that mastery of any craft includes, at minimum:

- Awareness of how the craft works

- Methods for practice and skill building

- Personal stakes that make personal change worthwhile[5]

THIS BOOK

Again, the key focus of this book is the craft of diversity management and, more specifically, its nature (the "awareness of how the craft works"); the need for achieving mastery of it in the context of personal, community, and organizational objectives (the awareness of "stakes that make change worthwhile"); and how mastery is achieved (the awareness of "methods for practice and skill building").

So, there is yet another reason why a leader may find this book of interest: It provides an opportunity to begin mastery of a craft that has received little attention yet offers great potential for achieving; sustaining; and, where possible, leveraging mixtures of differences and similarities in any dimension.

The five chapters in Part 2 of this book provide context by exploring personal, community, and organizational progress with diversity. The discussions of America as a diversity experiment, the Civil Rights Movement, and affirmative action highlight the need for (and potential benefits of) mastering the craft of diversity management. I will also recount the evolution of my own thinking about diversity.

The remainder of the book (Part 3) describes diversity management and the Strategic Diversity Management Process (SDMP)™, a step-by-step process that can be used to gain proficiency with SDM. We can think of SDM as the craft and SDMP as a key tool of the craft.

My hope is that you will find here an appreciation for SDM and begin to understand what it takes to master it. The potential of this craft for gains in personal, community, and organizational arenas is great. Once on the road to mastery, you will find that you are also on the path to achieving the next level of diversity effectiveness and fulfilling its promise.

PART TWO

CONTEXT

CHAPTER 2

THE UNITED STATES

AN EXPERIMENT IN DIVERSITY

FAMILIARITY BREEDS COMPLACENCY more often than contempt. Americans, accustomed to a nation where diverse peoples are united under "common rules of citizenship," to use Nathan Glazer's elegant phrase, take their system for granted.[1] Yet the United States may be unique in its diversity ideals and their accompanying challenges, and we're not doing well at meeting them.

Our forefathers, like all people who come together to launch a community, had to address several questions that we would define today as "diversity concerns" or "diversity questions." For example:

- Who could become citizens? How much and what kind of diversity (i.e., differences and similarities) should we have? How much—if any—assimilation should be required, and on what basis?

- How can we make certain that diverse citizens get along? What should we do about prejudice and discrimination? How do we encourage tolerance and understanding of differences?

- What type of government expectations and practices will empower *all* citizens?

This chapter looks at how the United States has answered these questions, the consequences of our choices, and the direction we might go from here. It explores the past, present, and future of what historian Arthur Schlesinger has called an experiment in a multiethnic society.[2]

The *Oxford English Dictionary* defines experiment as "a course of action tentatively adopted without being sure of the eventual outcome." This definition fits precisely with Schlesinger's view of the founding fathers' decision to include multiple ethnic and religious groups under one national umbrella. He describes this plan as a "bolder experiment than we sometimes remember," adding that "[h]istory is littered with the wreck of states that tried to combine diverse ethnic or linguistic or religious groups within a single sovereignty."[3] How successful has our nation's experiment in diversity been? That is the focus of this chapter.

THE PAST: HISTORICAL OVERVIEW

Many scholars and contemporary observers have written about the American Experiment as a multiethnic society. I view all these writings as being implicitly about diversity, even though they may not use the same vocabularies, and therefore I believe they have important ideas to contribute. In particular, I note the works of magazine editor Peter Brimelow; former secretary of the Department of Health, Education, and Welfare and founder of Common Cause John W. Gardner; sociologist Nathan Glazer; political scientist Samuel P. Huntington; historian Arthur M. Schlesinger; and journalist Benjamin Schwarz.

In numerous published works, these authors have examined America's answers to the diversity question and their impact on our national character. Using the lens of diversity management to interpret their commentary, I hope to expand our view of how the United States has approached diversity, what the consequences have been, and what diversity management challenges remain.

Foundational Diversity Decisions

Nathan Glazer argues that over time, three diversity decisions evolved. These decisions, he writes, ". . . were not taken all at once, or absolutely, or in full consciousness of their implications, but the major tendencies of American thought and political action have regularly given their assent to them."[4]

First, according to Glazer, "The entire world would be allowed to enter the United States," and the definition of an American would turn not on ethnicity, but rather on a "commitment to ideals" and a community defined by these ideals.[5] Second, he wrote, "No separate ethnic group was to be allowed to establish an independent polity in the United States." Third, "No group would be required to give up its group character and distinctiveness as the price of full entry into the American society and polity."[6]

Glazer sees the American Experiment as open to all. Yet this openness did not exist at the nation's founding. It emerged over a 200-year period.[7]

Benjamin Schwarz notes that the "American nationality was not a blending of all the peoples that populated the United States," but rather that of "a modified Englishman."[8]

Peter Brimelow agrees. He writes: "[T]he American nation has always had a specific ethnic core and that core has been white."[9] He also notes that when Thomas Paine wrote *Common Sense,* in which he called for America to be an "asylum for mankind," he meant an "asylum for *Europeans.*" Brimelow quotes Paine as proclaiming specifically, "We claim brotherhood with every European Christian."[10]

It was not until what Nathan Glazer calls "the consensus of the middle 1960s" that the United States settled on its current versions of the three diversity decisions.

Conditions for Success

One thing I am sure of: This consensus is always in flux. The diversity decisions delineated by Glazer don't manifest themselves in a vacuum. They can only be implemented if five conditions exist:

1. We must have consensus about the ideals that bind us. The greater this consensus, the easier it is to create an environment that works for all.

2. We must be open to change and willing to explore, continually and carefully, the appropriateness of existing values and ideals. Schlesinger writes, "The American identity will never be fixed and final; it will always be in the making." The challenge will be to permit this evolution without compromising "national integration."[11]

3. Citizens must assimilate willingly around the consensus ideals and values. A challenge (and significant source of diversity tension) is that encouragement to retain ethnic distinctiveness counters the needed assimilation.

4. Citizens must understand the "diversity decisions" and trust that they are operative if they are to support them. If they don't, fear of becoming a numerical minority will lead people to worry excessively about their parochial interests.

5. Citizens must possess the ability to manage diversity. That is, they must master the craft of making quality decisions amid the inevitable differences, similarities, and related tensions that result from welcoming all and allowing ethnic groups to retain their character.

If any of the five conditions is compromised, diversity tension escalates, along with the threat of contentious divisiveness. An ongoing compliance with these conditions is essential if the American Experiment is to succeed.

THE PRESENT: CURRENT STATE OF THE EXPERIMENT

As I write in 2005, divisiveness along a number of lines challenges the country. The five necessary conditions have been compromised, and we are clearly paying the price. This situation has existed for some time, including through the 1990s.

Commenting on the 1990s, Samuel P. Huntington noted intense debates on an impressive list of issues: "immigration and assimilation, multiculturalism and diversity, race relations and affirmative action, religion in the public sphere, bilingual education, school and college curricula, school prayer, abortion, the meaning of citizenship and nationality, foreign involvement in American elections, the extraterritorial applications of American law, and the increasing political role of diasporas here and abroad."[12]

About that same decade, John W. Gardner worried that cities in the United States were fragmented by "everything from momentary political battles to deep and complex ethnic rifts."[13]

A cursory review of today's media reveals that these observations remain valid midway through the new century's first decade. I am dismayed that not one of the five conditions necessary for the American Experiment's success is being met.

First, the country lacks consensus about the ideals that bind. Even the experts are at odds. Schlesinger, for example, worries that the notion of America as a place where all individuals are "melted into one people" has been compromised, replaced by a vision that espouses the protection, promotion, and preservation of "separate ethnic and racial communities." He attributes this to a "cult of ethnicity."[14]

Glazer refers to this new vision as "multiculturalism," which for him stems from America's failure to integrate blacks into the mainstream. Advocates of this perspective, he says, espouse "a new image [vision] of a better America without prejudice and discrimination, in which no cultural theme linked to any racial or ethnic group has priority, and in which American culture is seen as the product of a complex intermingle of themes from every minority, ethnic, and racial group and from indeed the whole world."[15]

Unlike Schlesinger, however, Glazer's prognosis is more benign. He does not see this multicultural development as threatening America's success story as "a diverse society that continues to welcome further diversity," but rather as pushing for inclusion under the American creed that dates back to the Constitution.[16] His view agrees with Schlesinger's position that the creed has been "the mechanism for translating diversity into unity."

Huntington disagrees with both Glazer and Schlesinger. He contends that since 1965, the glue for America has been its culture *and* creed, and that before 1965, ethnicity and race were also elements of the national identity. Huntington does not see American culture as ever-evolving, but believes that:

> America's core culture has been and is still primarily the culture of the seventeenth—and eighteenth—century settlers. The central elements include the Christian religion, Protestant values and moralism, a work ethic, the English language, British traditions of law, justice, and the limits of government power, and a legacy of European art, literature, philosophy, and music.[17]

The second condition for success—openness to change—is not being met, either. The number of contentious issues has not diminished with the dawning of a new century. In itself, the existence of conflict is not especially surprising. In a country that welcomes everyone, allows retention of ethnic character, and insists only on allegiance to the American creed, tensions around cultural changes are bound to surface.

What is surprising, and very troubling, is the level of divisiveness. The number, intensity, and tone of the disagreements are such that we call them "cultural *wars,*" suggesting that both civility and openness to mutual change are in very short supply. It also suggests that as a nation, we aren't ready for the challenges of diversity. This is distressing.

Tensions have always existed around the third condition—the willingness to assimilate. Today, multiculturalism and the "cult of ethnicity" offer an alternative vision to the assimilation metaphor of the melting pot.[18] The issue is not assimilation per se, but the reasoning behind it. Many people believe that assimilation is required in areas or ways that do not sufficiently reflect respect for ethnic, racial, and gender subcultures. They view America's core values as having an "Anglo-centric flavor," and since frustration with Anglo-centric-flavored assimilation historically has led to rejection of assimilation as desirable, they consider that a key barrier to achieving consensus.[19]

Their concerns take us back to a fundamental diversity issue: How can we achieve connectedness and cohesiveness? Some people point to the American creed. But this creed has not worked for African-Americans and, for a long time, was not even applied to them. Glazer points out that historical discussions about the "new man" being born through American assimilation rarely included blacks, even when they made up a significant portion of the country's population.[20]

Condition four is in disarray. I see little evidence that the public is aware of the American Experiment in diversity. Few people recognize and understand the "diversity decisions" or their implications. It is not widely known, for example, that America has been struggling with diversity and its inevitable tensions for more than 200 years, ever since its founding.

In particular, people are not clear about the evolutionary "work in progress" nature of their country's culture and how this reality flows from the diversity decision that ethnic character need not be abandoned. Yet, given that decision, how could American culture be anything other than a work in progress? It simply is not possible to welcome all ethnic groups to your house, require conformity only with specific parameters, and allow individuals to retain major aspects of their ethnicities and still be under no pressure for change.

Even citizens who are aware of the American Experiment and its fragile state are rarely eager to act. This may reflect a belief that a country that's more than 200 years old will prove immortal, or an inability to believe that the country still remains an experiment after 200 years, or a hope that "somebody else will deal with it."

It may also mean that people do not know how to enhance the American Experiment, or where to begin. Gardner, for example, asserts that the magnitude of the challenges facing the American city is not the major problem. The principal issue is "that it can't pull itself together to act on *any* of the issues. It cannot think as a community or act as a community."[21]

Or, to phrase that idea differently, I believe communities are not complying with the fifth condition for success—the requirement for diversity management. They have not mastered the craft of consistently making quality decisions when confronted with differences, similarities, and related tensions. They are not prepared for diversity or equipped to manage its challenges.

Certainly, we can find in communities healthy, vigorous efforts that promote racial and ethnic harmony and tolerance and minimize racial, ethnic, and gender discrimination and tension. Indeed, these programmatic thrusts often produce desirable and useful results. What they don't do, however, is equip citizens to *routinely* engage in effective decision making in the midst of diversity.

Given the limited awareness about the American Experiment in diversity, it is not surprising that neither the country nor its individual communities and citizens have acquired diversity management capabilities. Indeed, for some people, diversity is a politicized, dated concept that needs to be discarded. That serious thought can be given to abandoning a concept central to the country's history and future indicates the paltry understanding that exists about the issue.

THE FUTURE: WHOLENESS OR FRAGMENTATION

I believe the American Experiment is in a tattered state. The writings of Gardner, Glazer, Huntington, and Schlesinger suggest that they share this view. So how will we meet these significant challenges? What is the future to hold?

Gardner captures the essence of America's ongoing challenge when he identifies "wholeness incorporating diversity" as the "transcendent goal of our time." Clearly, our racial and ethnic groups must achieve integration. Yet, he warns, as we work toward that goal, leaders must act "to prevent wholeness from smothering diversity and to prevent the diversity from destroying the wholeness."[22]

This fine line must be negotiated if the American Experiment is to succeed. At issue: How can we best achieve this wholeness? Two conflicting views have come to the fore.

Return to the Settlers' Culture

Huntington identifies three ways in which a country can relate to the world:

1. *Cosmopolitan.* A country can embrace the world and allow its internal culture to be reshaped by external forces.

2. *Imperial.* A country can reshape world peoples and cultures in terms of its own culture.

3. *National.* A country can recognize, accept, and protect what distinguishes it from other societies.[23]

Huntington opts for the third worldview: a United States united around the reinvigoration of the country's "core" or Anglo-Protestant culture. For him, this "would mean a recommitment to America as a deeply religious and primarily Christian country, encompassing several religious minorities, adhering to Anglo-Protestant values, speaking English, maintaining its European cultural heritage, and committing to the principles of the Creed."[24] His argument: This has been America's culture from its settling and has served the country well. A national identity based on Anglo-Protestant culture would provide the integration glue for the United States "long after the WASPish descendants of its founders have become a small and uninfluential minority." So— and this point is critical—Huntington is arguing for the importance of the Anglo-Protestant *culture* and not Anglo-Protestant *people.*[25]

There are arguments in favor of and in opposition to Huntington's prescription. One positive is that the Anglo-Protestant culture enjoys historical familiarity and high esteem. At one time, most Americans would have eagerly vowed support for the components of this culture.

A significant negative is that the multicultural vision, which advocates respect and appreciation for *all* cultures, inherently challenges the Anglo-Protestant/European emphasis. Thus, by definition, America's current culture presents a serious barrier to adopting the Huntington prescription. Overcoming this thrust would prove difficult, contentious, and divisive.

A second negative is that it would be extremely difficult to advocate for the importance of Anglo-Protestant culture without seeming to argue for the importance of the Anglo-Protestant people. So this approach would appear exclusionary and would offend those who are not Anglo-Protestants. In a racially and ethnically sensitive society such as the United States, the potential for divisiveness would be substantial.

A third problem is that reinvigorating the Anglo-Protestant culture would compromise the "diversity decision" that allows retention of ethnic character. This decision may very well be embedded too deeply in America's current culture to allow a return to the settlers' culture.

These powerful negatives make it highly unlikely that Huntington's prescription will take hold. The Anglo-Protestant culture is probably not as strong as Huntington presumes. The work in progress, for better or worse, may be beyond the point of return.

The Multicultural Alternative

Both Glazer and Schlesinger argue for a unifying culture that is multicultural in nature—one culture that encompasses all subcultures. Schlesinger calls for a renewing of allegiance to the unifying ideals that already exist as a means to prevent differences from escalating into antagonisms and hatred.[26] Glazer calls for restraint, endorsing the view that Americans should "have respect for identity in the context of . . . [our existing] common culture" while avoiding fixed "lines of division on ethnic and racial basis."[27]

The critical idea in support of the multicultural alternative is that it preserves the diversity decisions and sets the stage for progress toward success with the American Experiment. It also builds on what already exists. Unfortunately, there is an overwhelming difficulty with this prescription: lack of clarity and specifics about implementation. Both Glazer and Schlesinger provide helpful analyses about multiculturalism but few particulars about implementation.

IN CONCLUSION . . .

How shall we choose between multiculturalism and Huntington's vision of a reinvigorated Anglo-Protestant culture? In my view, multiculturalism is decidedly more viable because it encourages the pursuit of the American Experiment as it has been historically defined. Nonetheless, two of Huntington's cautions, while not necessarily valid, deserve attention.

First, Huntington worries that "a multicultural America will, in time, become a multicreedal America, with groups with different cultures espousing distinctive political values and principles rooted in their particular cultures." Second, he states that "the makings of serious white nativist movements and of intensified racial conflict exist in America."[28]

Even though I may not accept Huntington's predictions (unlike Huntington, I believe that returning to the settlers' culture would do more to fan these flames than multiculturalism), they have value in that they force us to be aware of potential pitfalls. We must take pains to implement the multicultural option carefully and thoroughly, making sure that all subcultures are reflected in the one unifying culture. For this to happen in practice, several things must occur.

First, we cannot assume that the American Experiment and the diversity decisions are the will of the land. Civic leaders must encourage affirmation of these ideas. They must engage in meaningful, informative, and even inspiring dialogue at national, state, and local levels to instill in the American people a deep appreciation of the American Experiment's history and nature, and an awareness of alternatives to it. Our civic leaders must also affirm that, when all is said and done, we must move forward cohesively. The ultimate goal: to equip citizens for informed decision making and—if the American Experiment is affirmed—implementation.

Second, civic leaders must help citizens to understand and affirm the conditions for the success of the American Experiment and their implications. They should, for example, emphasize that conscious, deliberate, persistent effort is required for implementation. If not nurtured intensely and continuously, the experiment will wane. They must also emphasize that cautious but real openness to change is essential for success of the American Experiment.

Third, they must support the development of a diversity management capability. By themselves, good intentions won't bring the American Experiment to successful fruition. Collective and individual mastery of the craft of making quality decisions in the midst of diversity is an absolute must. Indeed, pursuing this capability before (or at least simultaneously with) the affirmation dialogue would enhance the success of the diversity conversations.

Finally, both leaders and individual citizens should refuse to be discouraged by the back-and-forth, up-and-down fluctuations that come with efforts to implement the American Experiment. We must remember that our country, its culture, and our collective mastery of the diversity management craft are works in progress. No doubt, much work remains.

THE CIVIL RIGHTS MOVEMENT

IN PURSUIT OF THE "BELOVED COMMUNITY"

DIVERSITY AND THE CIVIL RIGHTS MOVEMENT are not the same thing. Nor is diversity, as an issue for America in the twenty-first century, an outgrowth of the movement, a successor, or a descendant. If we are to fully understand diversity and diversity management, and take advantage of their powerful capacity for change, we must separate them from the legacy of the Civil Rights Movement.

Many people are disquieted by that statement, so I wish to start by making my own position clear.

Without question, the civil rights struggles of the 1950s, 1960s, and 1970s, embodied in what is generally referred to as "the movement," are a powerful part of our communal history. There is no question that the goals of that movement are not fully realized; as a nation, we have more to do.

Many people hold a deeply personal, deeply emotional allegiance to the movement and recoil at any suggestion that seems to contradict its values. When I argue that diversity comprises a wide array of mixtures and thus predates the Civil Rights Movement, these individuals often hear something else. They perceive this definition of diversity as a distraction from a focus that should be on social justice—or worse, as a haven for racism—and they want nothing to do with it.

Let there be no doubt about this: As an African-American who grew up in the South during that time, I honor the Civil Rights Movement and what it means for all Americans. When I say that understanding diversity and diversity management requires a mental and emotional separation from the Civil Rights Movement, I am speaking from a position of profound gratitude and respect for the pioneers of that movement. Whenever I think of all that is embodied in that movement, I realize how deeply indebted we all are to these individuals.

Yet as I travel around the country talking about diversity, I regularly encounter people who confuse the two, and that confusion makes it difficult for them to embrace diversity and diversity management in their fullest sense. This confusion is evident wherever people equate "diversity" with:

- An extension of the Civil Rights Movement

- The pursuit of racial and social justice

- Affirmative action and racial desegregation

- Something that involves race and gender

- A concept in which white males have no role

These misperceptions make it difficult for people to learn the craft of diversity management, which means they are missing out on the enormous potential it offers in a multitude of arenas—*including* the civil rights agenda.

This chapter examines, in overview, the Civil Rights Movement from the perspective of diversity and diversity management. In so doing, we look at the assumptions about diversity contained within the civil rights agenda and explore how diversity management can facilitate accomplishing that agenda.

THE BELOVED COMMUNITY: THE PROTOTYPICAL CIVIL RIGHTS IDEAL

Three schools of thought exist about the Civil Rights Movement. In one, people see the movement as a historical relic that refuses to fade away.

A second group of people look at the movement's history and

say, "Much remains to be done." Their reasoning: "Our ultimate goals were participation in the mainstream and equal opportunity for blacks. We're not there yet."

People who adhere to a third school of thought say, "We've made significant progress with desegregation, but our ultimate goal is the integrated community or organization. We must move toward Dr. Martin Luther King's ideal of an enlightened society, symbolized by what came to be known as the 'Beloved Community.'"[1]

This chapter focuses on the third approach, for one simple reason: Despite their differences, members of all three schools share a common commitment and loyalty to the ideal of the Beloved Community. The decision to use Dr. King's philosophy as the comparison arena should in no way be viewed as minimizing the contributions of others to the movement. I have chosen to frame the chapter around the Beloved Community because its broad appeal makes it an excellent domain for exploring the relationship among diversity, diversity management, and the Civil Rights Movement.

EVOLUTION OF THE BELOVED COMMUNITY

The Beloved Community represented for Dr. King the desired integrated community. The thrust for integration, however, predates him. Its genesis can be traced back at least to the Reconstruction era after the Civil War. However, it was Dr. King who in the 1950s and 1960s fleshed out and popularized the notion of integration as the heart of the Beloved Community.

The word *integration* did not officially surface until after World War I. However, if we define integration as full participation in the mainstream, its evolution actually began during the Reconstruction era when the United States Congress passed a series of acts intended to grant full citizenship to former slaves.[2]

This initial congressional action did not last long. In 1883, The U.S. Supreme Court declared the Civil Rights Act of 1875 unconstitutional. In 1896, in *Plessy* v. *Ferguson*, the court ruled that blacks had no rights that whites were obligated to recognize. Southern legislators quickly enacted "Jim Crow laws" segregating the races.[3]

In 1905, W.E.B. DuBois responded to this lost ground by spear-heading the Niagara movement for the purposes of attacking the legal disenfranchisement of blacks and the Jim Crow doctrine of separate but equal.[4] The movement was short-lived, and DuBois joined with other former members to form the National Negro Committee, which in 1909 became the National Association for the Advancement of Colored People (NAACP). The newly created organization adopted integration as its "official agenda."[5]

Between the two world wars, as the NAACP continued its stand for integration against white resistance and black doubt, its lawyers formally introduced the word in internal documents. "Integration" meant breaking down Jim Crow barriers to full citizenship by achieving racial mingling. The NAACP's efforts were not successful, however, and the world noticed.

In 1944, the Swedish sociologist Gunnar Myrdal wrote *An American Dilemma,* accusing the United States of denying former slaves the racial equality inherent in what he termed the American creed. This creed, in Myrdal's words, consisted of "the ideals of the essential dignity of the individual, of the basic equality of all men, and of certain inalienable rights to freedom, justice, and fair opportunity." This hypocrisy-grounded dilemma, Myrdal felt, could threaten the allegiance of blacks and their willingness to fight for the United States.[6] In his view, America was caught between its claim of practicing democracy, its denial of democracy's privileges to blacks, and the growing resentment of the descendants of former slaves.[7]

Following World War II, the United States became concerned about Myrdal's indictment and its implications for the country's image. In addition, the fact that blacks had fought in World War II for racial tolerance and democratic values that they did not enjoy at home heightened white awareness and sensitivity to the sting of Myrdal's accusations. These combined factors made race a moral issue and set the stage for President Harry Truman's civil rights efforts.[8]

Truman's actions in the late 1940s gave integration advocates hope. He appointed the President's Committee on Civil Rights, which issued a report describing violence, discrimination, and exploitation against blacks as pervasive forms of social, political, and economic policies. Most important, he issued an executive order ending discrimination in the armed services and in federal employment. By that order, he desegregated these organizations.

Myrdal's indictment made race, segregation, desegregation, and integration moral issues. The "school desegregation case" of 1954 (*Oliver L. Brown et al.* v. *Board of Education of Topeka*) placed them in a psychological perspective. In pursuing the case against school desegregation, NAACP lawyers used a major research finding by psychologist Kenneth Clark that racial separation, in and of itself, caused blacks to feel inferior. This report significantly influenced the thinking of the justices.[9]

In the battle over racial mixing in America's public schools, both advocates and resisters used the terms *desegregation* and *integration* interchangeably.[10] It was Dr. King who differentiated between the two, in a 1962 speech entitled "The Ethical Demands for Integration." In the same speech, he challenged the view that integration was not an end in itself, but rather a means to an end (full participation). His views about his faith and the nature of humanity convinced him that integration in and of itself had to be the "ultimate goal."[11]

In his speech, King said that desegregation and the resulting racial pluralism were not enough. Even with 100 percent desegregation, he said, the human relations dilemma would remain unless the country simultaneously pursued integration, which he defined as "the positive acceptance of desegregation and the welcomed participation of Negroes into the total range of human activities." Integration was "genuine intergroup, interpersonal doing," and the ultimate goal of our international community.[12]

To make the distinction between the terms clearer, he went on to say that integration was spiritual whereas desegregation by itself was "physical proximity without spiritual affinity." Dr. King felt that after desegregation, "something must touch the hearts and souls of men so that they will come together spiritually because it is natural and right."[13] He believed that three ethical demands required integration and not simply desegregation:

1. The Worth of Individuals (Everybody is somebody.)

2. Life's Demands for Freedom (Denial of freedom—the capacity to deliberate, decide, and respond—is a denial of life.)

3. The Unity of Humanity (We are all one and created by the same Creator.)[14]

These "ethical demands" give legitimacy to the need for integration and also specify the nature of the integration required. In that regard, Dr. King's view of the integrated community becomes the undergirding core of the Beloved Community. The higher the quality of integration—that is, the greater the adherence to the ethical demands—the closer we come to the Beloved Community.

This is a most significant development. Dr. King was saying that integration, the reconciliation of man across lines of race, nations, and creeds, is—indeed, morally has to be—the ultimate goal. Desegregation—the removal of laws sanctioning segregation—was *one* step toward that end but by itself was inadequate. To achieve the goal of integration, Dr. King said, the United States must look beyond racial mingling (i.e., racial pluralism) to quality race relations.

Dr. King's thinking was always evolving. In the speech on the ethical demands for integration, where he argued effectively that integration had to be the "ultimate goal," he also simultaneously implied that it was not. He argued that "community" (i.e., civilization) was the ultimate goal, and it required integration. For Dr. King, the universe was so structured that things would not work out right if individuals were not "diligent in their concern for others."[15] Because this diligence required integration, the sequential ordering for Dr. King was:

Racial Segregation   →   Racial Desegregation   →

Racial Pluralism   →   Racial Integration   →

Beloved Community

In essence, Dr. King sought in this particular speech to warn the country about the challenge of melding community in the midst of racial differences, similarities, and tensions (although the vocabulary is mine, not his). Without the spiritual connectedness that integration requires, there would be no community, and chaos would become a real possibility. Settling for desegregation alone was no longer an option.

Interestingly, Dr. King's three ethical pillars for integration parallel Myrdal's description of the three tenets of the American creed. Essentially, then, he argued in this 1962 speech that the integration foundation for the Beloved Community should be the American creed.

Given the frequency with which civil rights advocates and others refer to the Beloved Community, I had expected that somewhere in his writings and speeches Dr. King had detailed clearly the nature of this ideal. Instead, I had difficulty locating his comments on the topic. In reality, Dr. King spoke neither frequently nor clearly about the Beloved Community. In fact, as Fredrik Sunnemark, a historian at Sweden's University Trollhättan-Uddevalla, notes in *Ring Out Freedom,* "The term is always vague to the point where it almost seems empty. It describes the happy situation when the present society has been rid of all its evils; it is the end result of the struggle waged."[16]

Why, then, does the concept enjoy popularity beyond its prominence in Dr. King's works? Several reasons:

■   Its vagueness allows people with a variety of views to subscribe to it. As such, it becomes an integrative "big tent" for a wide range of civil rights advocates and supporters.

■   The concept embraces and goes beyond the ideal (something that we actively and consciously strive for and that can be achieved under the best of circumstances) but is not utopia (something that influences the nature of the ideal but is not achievable). Sunnemark states that for Dr. King, the kingdom of God was utopia. He contends further that the Beloved Community, as evolved by Dr. King, is the "name" given to the results of combining the kingdom of God with a reformed America.[17] As a consequence of this mixing, the *Beloved Community* term offers inspiration and guidance.

■   Although Dr. King rarely spoke specifically and deeply about the concept of the Beloved Community, his life and goals did. At times, when reading his work, people say, in the awe of discovery, "*That's what he means by the 'Beloved Community.'*" That was certainly my reaction while reading "The Ethical Demands for Integration."

■   A final reason for the Beloved Community's enduring popularity is that it refers to a "world community." Long before globalism and its implications became topical, Dr. King described "civil rights" as "God-given" and available to *all* humanity of *all* nationalities, races, and creeds. He believed that a "world perspective" was essential to achieving the American Dream.[18] This global feature enhances the present relevance of the Beloved Community concept.

PRINCIPAL PARAMETERS OF THE BELOVED COMMUNITY

Goal. The goal is the Beloved Community through racial integration, as articulated by Dr. King.

Critical Concepts. The central concepts, and their definitions, include:

■   *Racial Oppression.* Disenfranchisement of, or discrimination against, a group because of its race.

■   *Equal Opportunity.* Freedom of individuals to reach their full potential without artificial barriers, such as racial oppression.

■   *Racial Segregation.* Legal sanctioning for the separation of the races, or the prohibition of racial mingling.

■   *Racial Desegregation.* Removal of legal sanctions for the separation of the races, such as elimination of Jim Crow laws.

■   *Racial Pluralism.* The presence of multiple races in a mixture, which is what you would expect to follow racial desegregation.

■   *Racial Awareness and Sensitivity.* A condition where people are alert to how their attitudes and behaviors can hamper development of productive relationships with members of other races.

■   *Racial Integration.* Spiritual bonding or connectedness among people from different races within the context of Dr. King's ethical demands for integration.

Facilitators of Integration. Recall the ethical demands for integration articulated by Dr. King:
1. Everybody is somebody.
2. Life demands freedom.
3. We are all one and created by the same Creator.

As noted previously, these demands correspond to the American creed as delineated by Gunnar Myrdal, who cited:
1. The essential dignity of the individual
2. The basic equality of all men
3. Inalienable rights to freedom, justice, and fair opportunity

Current Status. Civil rights advocates appear to be stuck on desegregation and racial pluralism, not sure how best to move to the next level in pursuit of the Beloved Community. They also use the words *desegregation* and *integration* interchangeably and define desegregation as racial pluralism. In sum, they are unclear about the concepts of racial desegregation, racial pluralism, and racial integration, which probably contributes to the stuck condition.

Unfinished Business. Racial integration in the spirit of Dr. King's thinking has yet to be achieved. Indeed, some civil rights supporters and others are ambivalent about the desirability of integration. This ambivalence, which dates back to the mid-1800s, is also part of the unfinished business.[19]

Barriers. The reality that people across lines of race and ethnicity do not subscribe fully to Dr. King's ethical demands for integration or, for that matter, the American creed, presents a major challenge. In the absence of widespread commitment, the demands lose their punch.

Another barrier is the continuation of racist attitudes and behavior. Dr. King came to recognize that racism would generate considerable resistance to the Beloved Community. This differs markedly from his view in the 1950s that "most Americans were committed to racial justice, and that although some white Southerners and a smattering of racist Northerners were bigots, the Civil Rights Movement was 'touching the conscious of America.'" Dr. King later concluded that "most Americans are unconscious racists" and that genuine commitment to genuine equality for Negroes has never been solid on the part of the vast majority of white Americans.[20]

A final barrier is the reality of differences. Civil rights advocates, by necessity, emphasized similarities as they sought to make their case for equality. A good example is Dr. King's observation that we are all one and have the same Creator. It is not that this statement and similar ones are false. They simply omit or downplay the reality of differences.

Desired End. Amid racial differences, similarities, and tensions, all individuals are welcomed and enjoy respect, equal opportunity, and a sense of spiritual unity and connectedness with *all* members of the Beloved Community. The foundation is Dr. King's "ethical demands" for integration.

THE BELOVED COMMUNITY, INTEGRATION, AND DIVERSITY MANAGEMENT

Implicit and explicit in the Beloved Community is the notion that diversity embraces all races, nationalities, and creeds. The Beloved Community simply *requires* integration in the mix. While few people would argue with Dr. King's ethical demands for integration, equally few are clear about how to achieve this integration. Indeed, at the time of his death, Dr. King struggled with the issue of how best to make progress. This is the heart of the Beloved Community's unfinished business.

The craft of diversity management offers enormous potential at this junction. It is a mechanism for achieving integration based on the ethical dimensions. In fact, it is difficult to see how integration that incorporates these ethical demands can be achieved without a diversity management capability.

This capability would offer civil rights activists a process for analysis and integration. It would encourage clarity about the amount of diversity they have and the amount they desire, and about the amount of connectedness they have and the amount that they want. It would also encourage productive dialogue about the basis on which this connectedness is to be built. Most important, it would offer a guide for meeting these goals while adhering to the ethical criteria embedded in the Beloved Community.

Leaders who desire to bring about progress, whether at the local, state, or national level, or in organizations, can do the following:

■ *Engage in and encourage dialogue about the Civil Rights Movement and the Beloved Community.* Among the questions needing attention are: What is our conceptual understanding of the Civil Rights Movement and the Beloved Community? What progress have we made with racial issues? What remains to be done? What are our aspirations? Do we wish to pursue the Beloved Community?

There are no right or wrong answers. What's important is to establish an accurate assessment of where a given community or organization is with respect to racial issues, the Civil Rights Movement, and the Beloved Community, and where it wishes to go. This dialogue should create a readiness for going to the next level.

■ *Gain an operational understanding of the Beloved Community.* What is required to achieve the Beloved Community? What are the operational and implementation implications of Dr. King's ethical demands for integration?

■ *Seek conceptual and operational clarity about diversity and diversity management.* How do their concepts differ from those associated with the Civil Rights Movement and the Beloved Community? How do these concepts play themselves out in our setting? How can diversity management complement efforts to achieve integration based on Dr. King's ethical demands?

■ *Communicate understandings, conclusions, and aspirations about the Civil Rights Movement and diversity management through-*

out the community or organization. The goal is to secure across-the-board buy-in.

■   *Take the necessary steps to master the craft of diversity management as a community or an organization.* The craft of Strategic Diversity Management™ is presented in Part 3 of this book as a framework for addressing diversity. Leaders can use this craft in pursuit of integration and the Beloved Community.

IN CONCLUSION . . .

Underlying all these suggestions is one fundamental premise: that diversity management can help advance the civil rights/Beloved Community agenda. Most of the suggestions cited here are designed to bring about a mind-set shift from the pejorative, misinformed rhetoric about diversity. For most leaders, this mind-set shift will prove an enormous, necessary first step toward mastering the craft of Strategic Diversity Management in pursuit of the Beloved Community.

CHAPTER 4

DIVERSITY AND AFFIRMATIVE ACTION

PAST, PRESENT, AND FUTURE

IN 1997, A YOUNG WHITE WOMAN was denied admission to the University of Michigan Law School partly on the basis of race. The resulting legal action eventually reached the Supreme Court (*Grutter v. Bollinger et al.*), which in 2003 decided, on a five-to-four vote, that the school's admission policy was in fact constitutional.

The school never denied that race was one aspect of the selection process but argued that it was a deliberate strategy for achieving diversity among the student body and the educational benefits that diversity would bring.

The justices apparently agreed. They noted the highly individualized reviews that each application received and concluded that the intensive review process ensured that *all* the factors in an applicant's background that could contribute to diversity—not merely race—were considered, and thus race was not in itself a determinant for either acceptance or rejection. Therefore, the court concluded, "The race-conscious admissions program does not unduly harm nonminority applicants."[1]

Two points stand out. It seems clear that the justices accepted the idea that diversity, per se, makes a contribution to a person's education. It is also clear that their definition of diversity is not limited to race.

One further item from this case, particularly relevant to this chapter, is found in Justice Sandra Day O'Connor's remarks. Speaking for the majority, she said, "Twenty-five years from now, the use of racial preferences will no longer be necessary to further the interest [pursuit of diversity] approved today."[2]

How should we interpret that remark? Was it nothing more than a figure of speech, representing a parallel reference to the twenty-five years that had elapsed since the previous pivotal affirmative action case (*Regents of University of California* v. *Bakke*), when racial quotas were essentially eliminated but the use of race as a "plus factor" in selection processes was allowed? Or was it a precise calculation for a specific timetable, a warning that the court would rescind its approval of affirmative action by 2028?

Advocates on all sides have debated Justice O'Connor's meaning. Some ignore this statement; some view it as one person's hope for the future. Others see it as a quasi-guarantee that affirmative action will be legally acceptable for another twenty-five years. Still others interpret it as an admonishment to leaders to begin developing legitimate alternatives against the day when affirmative action will be disallowed.

Those who believe that affirmative action's time is limited are of three minds. Some people believe that discontinuing it—whenever that might be—would be a mistake. Others see discontinuation as long overdue. Still others see affirmative action as a current necessity whose life expectancy is limited.

I am in the third group, and I am concerned. America has not used wisely the time that affirmative action has bought us. To discontinue it today would result in divisiveness, conflict, and turmoil.

We must spend the grace time that has been given to eliminate the *need* for affirmative action. That means that we must *collectively figure out how to achieve the desired racial representation within America's institutions without resorting to race-conscious tools*. Only then can we discontinue affirmative action without inviting chaos.

This changeover won't be easy. Few measures in our society have triggered as much controversy, with plaudits and resentment in almost equal measure. Proponents on both sides remain passionate in their convictions. Further complicating honest debate is the fact that affirmative action is also the most widely recognizable point where diversity and politics intersect. When I say that diversity, in its broadest sense, has become politicized and therefore fractious and divisive, affirmative action policies are what come to mind most often. It is the one facet commonly related to diversity that triggers the fiercest emotions and the most contentious debates.

Ironically, this political intertwining has hindered the ability to move to the next level and simultaneously fostered the need to do so. It has hindered progress by generating heat and divisiveness at the same time as the legal maneuverings have created pressure to move forward.

BEGINNINGS: AN OVERVIEW

President Lyndon Johnson's 1965 Executive Order 11246 prescribed affirmative action as affirmative efforts "to ensure that all qualified applicants and employees receive equal employment opportunity."[3] Although affirmative action became crystallized with this order, it is not something created by a single act. It is, instead, an aggregate of directives, administrative guidelines, and court decisions, all of which were intended to expedite the integration ("mainstreaming") of African-Americans into America's institutions.[4]

This expediting was necessary because the United States was not ready for diversity. When the Civil Rights Act of 1964 passed into law, joining previous court cases that had challenged laws sanctioning racial discrimination, *desegregation* became the legal order of the day. These developments resulted in "color-blind law" that prohibited distinctions on the basis of race, color, religion, or national origin, with respect to the provision of public services and the right to public employment and public education.[5] Implicit in this requirement that no account be given to race, color, religion, or national origin is an enhanced emphasis on individual rights as opposed to group rights.

Theoretically, these legal shifts greatly increased the racial diversity of the pool of *potential* employees, yet workforce representation for African-Americans stayed low and advancement for those few already in the pipeline was minimal. It became clear that eliminating legal discrimination would not bring significant progress quickly.

The underlying reason—even though we did not then have the vocabulary to express it fully—was that America's organizations, collectively and individually, lacked the wherewithal to manage racial diversity. Organizations, and the people within them, had not yet learned the diversity skills or achieved the diversity maturity they would need. Few corporate cultures could facilitate the mainstreaming of minorities, and institutional barriers were commonplace.

Those intent on having African-Americans benefit quickly from the new law were doubly frustrated to find that many of these institutional barriers did not constitute discrimination as defined by the civil rights laws. They became convinced that something above and beyond the Civil Rights Act was needed. Affirmative action was that something. The purpose was not to eliminate institutional barriers, which everyone realized was a long-term effort, but rather to get around them—to provide a transitional Band-Aid until the prescription of legal color blindness could facilitate the mainstreaming of African-Americans.

Initial efforts relied on "outreach" affirmative action—that is, identifying and recruiting qualified or qualifiable African-Americans.[6] Eventually, however, more specific goals and target requirements were added. Advocates believed that "institutional racism (intentional or not)" dictated the need for these "racial preference" remedies.[7]

These remedies represented a dramatic shift from the Civil Rights Act's emphasis on color blindness, desegregation, and individual rights. They focused instead on color consciousness, integration, and group representation.[8]

Not everyone was happy. Activists in the Civil Rights Movement had been united in seeking a color-blind society in which the nation would finally fulfill the 100-year-old promise of the Emancipation Proclamation. However, former compatriots split over affirmative action. Those who still sought color blindness and individual rights were appalled by affirmative action, believing that its race consciousness directly contradicted the Constitution and civil rights laws.[9] They were "astonished to find themselves governed by quotas which were prohibited by the Civil Rights Act of 1964."[10] Civil rights activists who supported affirmative action were equally appalled at the snail's pace at which integration was proceeding under the Civil Rights Act. They were willing to try whatever might work.

Many of the arguments that raged in the 1960s are alive and well today and, now as then, exist within an atmosphere that is intensely political. Indeed, affirmative action not only remains political; it has become politicized. In politicized conversations, as opposed to political ones, the debate is not about the merits of the issue. It is about governance power.

This politicization (and subsequent focus on power) brings troubling consequences. For one, it has reduced the motivation to develop alternatives and complements to affirmative action, because the debate is less about the merits of alternatives than about the disinclination to relinquish power. It has also created confusion about diversity by defining it as a code word for affirmative action. This, in turn, has hampered the evolution and acceptance of diversity management as a concept and a process.

Our collective understanding of affirmative action's intent has become murky as well. One point in particular has gotten lost in all the verbal jousting: Affirmative action was a vehicle for increasing the representation (i.e., presence) of African-Americans in the mainstreams of U.S. life for the benefit of *society,* not organizations. Anything we do now to complement or provide alternatives to affirmative action must be grounded on an accurate understanding of this historical purpose. Persuasive arguments, both pro and con, must meet this requirement as well.

THE CASE FOR AFFIRMATIVE ACTION

Affirmative action advocates offer various justifications for its continuation. As in the beginning, however, they tend to focus on ways to get around the problem rather than address it directly. That is, they deal with the inability of America's institutions to adapt adequately to the increased diversity in workforce and educational pools and thus neglect the urgent need to remediate the inadequacies that prevent these institutions from adapting well. Let's analyze some of the justifications used by advocates to make the case for affirmative action.

Justification 1: Affirmative action is necessary to foster equal opportunity. This means giving people "an equal chance to compete within the framework of goals and the structure of rules established by our particular society. . . ."[11]

My Observation. Equal opportunity does not address the conditions of competition. Imagine an African-American who is admitted to a game without being told the rules and having to compete with those who understand the rules. He may have equal access, but he does not have equal opportunity.

Affirmative action has not addressed this issue. True equal opportunity would require removing barriers that disadvantage African-Americans. In particular, attention should be given to those barriers that are not absolute requirements for strategic success, such as traditions, preferences, and conveniences that fall into this category. If these nonrequirement barriers were removed, genuine equal opportunity could be achieved.

Justification 2: Affirmative action is needed to foster equality of results (statistical parity integration). People who make this argument believe one or all of the following:

- Inequalities in the opportunity to compete will always exist. Therefore, we should focus on equality of results.
- The destructive competitiveness that characterizes organizations allows some people to reap disproportionate rewards while others starve.
- If equal access could be achieved, new inequalities based on "accidents" of talent would emerge, and they would be no fairer than any others.[12]

My Observation. John Gardner has noted that American society has difficulty with the "equality of results" argument. Some rewards relate not to "accidents" but to performance based on perseverance, character, and loyalty. Conversely, some poor performances are the result of laziness and irresponsibility. Americans wish to retain the option of differentiating between such performances.[13] I am comfortable with Gardner's view.

Justification 3: Affirmative action is needed to compensate those who have been discriminated against. Proponents argue that America uniquely deprived African-Americans to the degree that compensation will be required for many years. They view affirmative action as a way to level the playing field and/or an entitlement repayment for the "sins of the past."[14]

My Observation. This argument positions affirmative action as a vehicle for extending reparations to African-Americans. However, I find few whites are even aware of the reparations debate, or are willing to accept responsibility for their ancestors' sins. The likelihood of this justification gaining substantial support appears to be slim.[15]

Justification 4: Affirmative action is needed to fight poverty. This argument was peripheral to the original discussions about affirmative action, but it has grown in significance over the years.

My Observation. The need to fight poverty was one reason for launching affirmative action. But its core purpose was to bypass gradualism and to get African-Americans mainstreamed as quickly as possible—because it was *morally right* to do so.

People who don't know about this distinction feel resentful and confused when people who are already well off gain financially from affirmative action. But they have missed the point. In the context of the original thinking, it is vulnerability to barriers, not poverty, that necessitates affirmative action, whether those barriers are illegal or legal but unnecessary. A "wealthy" minority may be just as vulnerable to institutional barriers as a "poor" minority.

Justification 5: Affirmative action is desirable to create role models. In some organizations, it has become commonplace to suggest that poor performance is connected to lack of role models. Some managers, therefore, advocate using affirmative action to recruit African-Americans from outside the organization for senior posts or the fast track. Once on board, they become "models" for other African-Americans, demonstrating what is possible as they assume their responsibilities and move up the ladder.[16]

My Observation. This argument works only when minorities and women trust the system. Without that trust, this technique only serves to cast doubt about the organization's commitment to its employees and about whether the environment would work without affirmative action. "If affirmative action were not in place," people wonder, "would the company still care about people like me?" It also sends the message that the goal is to create role models, rather than to question whether the current system works for all.

Justification 6: Affirmative action is required to foster diversity. Proponents believe that affirmative action can bring about racial, ethnic, and gender diversity that, in turn, will foster creativity and innovation. Another, related argument is that it will foster the diversity needed to pursue diverse racial, ethnic, and gender markets.

My Observation. Subscribers to this rationale should recognize that diversity is not a magic pill that will suddenly solve the organization's market problems. Remember, diversity is inherently neither good nor bad. It simply is. Its potential for positive change, innovation, or stagnation depends on the situation, the nature of the diversity, and the ability of individuals to make quality decisions amid differences, similarities, and tension. If anything is inherently good, it is the craft of diversity management.

This rationale is part of the effort to prove the merits of a diverse workforce. It implies that if I cannot prove diversity will benefit your organization, you as a manager can ignore it. The reality is that whether or not there are benefits, organizations already do have a diverse workforce—and always will. Diversity is a reality.

Another problem with this rationale is that it presumes that the most important argument for affirmative action is its potential benefits for an organization or community. Not so. The overarching case for affirmative action is that mainstreaming minorities and women benefits the whole of American society, independent of the impact on communities or organizations.

A critical presumption implicit in this justification is that organizations can make quality decisions in the midst of the diversity that affirmative action generates. But if organizations cannot *manage* that diversity, potential gains will elude them and perhaps even become liabilities.

THE CASE AGAINST AFFIRMATIVE ACTION

Opponents of affirmative action have been equally industrious in developing their justifications. Let's analyze some of these arguments as well.

Argument 1: Affirmative action departs from the ideal of a color-blind society before the law.[17] For these individuals, this ideal represents the essence of what the Civil Rights Movement has been about, whereas affirmative action, with its consideration of color, has meant a step backward and the potential loss of a hard-earned gain. Accordingly, proponents strongly believe it is important to resist affirmative action.

My Observation. True. However, neither antidiscrimination laws nor programs for minorities do much to eliminate the legal and illegal institutional barriers that spurred the evolution of affirmative action.

Argument 2: Affirmative action fosters reverse discrimination. Proponents of this view contend that racial problems have been solved and that most of our current racial friction is caused by racial and gender preferences that work to displace "qualified" whites, usually males.[18] They make no distinction between acts of discrimination that produce harm and those intended to remedy or restore.[19] Discrimination, they say, is discrimination. They count on color-blind law and policy to lead to a color-blind society.

My Observation. I agree that discrimination is discrimination, but past history indicates that color-blind laws and policies aren't enough by themselves. This argument would be more compelling if it were accompanied by effective plans for alleviating the continuing impact of previous acts.

Argument 3: Affirmative action is divisive in its insistence on determining who is disadvantaged. This insistence leads to the drawing of group definitions, thus making group conflicts more likely. People who make this argument also believe that affirmative action compromises the traditional vision of a unified United States in a way that affects politics, volunteer organizations, the nation's religious organizations, and its language.[20]

My Observation. This argument may be ascribing too much significance to affirmative action. Fundamentally, affirmative action focuses not on the disadvantaged in general, but specifically on African-Americans who have been discriminated against historically. That doesn't mean that we should not seek to assist the disadvantaged in general; it simply means that it is not the historical purpose of affirmative action.

Furthermore, societal fragmentation today stems largely from our failure to emphasize and gain consensus about the similarities (i.e., the ties that bind) necessary for continuing unity. We must become more effective in this regard.

Argument 4: Affirmative action stigmatizes the beneficiaries and makes it difficult for them to gain respect for their accomplishments. Yale Law School professor Stephen Carter, for example, resents affirmative action because it denied him the opportunity to know whether he could make it on his own.[21]

My Observation. Many people who have benefited from affirmative action share this feeling, and so the criticism has some validity. But it also raises the question, Does anybody make it on their own or solely on merit? My research has convinced me that "merit" has three components: task proficiency, cultural compatibility, and political support. To advance in a given organization, people must competently dispatch their assigned responsibilities, fit in sufficiently with the enterprise's culture, and attract ample political support from people with the power to make the "merit" case. Very few people make it on their own. Some kind of assistance, deserved or not, comes into play, solicited or not.

Argument 5: Managers, politicians, and others have abused affirmative action, thus corrupting it. Proponents here argue that the process has been corrupted and therefore should be abolished. Regardless of intent, its credibility has been tarnished beyond repair.

My Observation. To some extent, this contention is true, reprehensible, and damaging to the legitimacy of affirmative action. However, it is not reason enough to abandon the Band-Aid effect that affirmative action provides until we have a prescription and process for achieving the desired state.

THE PRESENT

At present, affirmative action operates amid these conflicts and the uncertainty of recent court judgments. Those who oppose affirmative action believe it is on its last legs. Those who favor it are encouraged by its historical resilience. No one knows what will happen next.

We do know, however—or should—that it is vital to avoid the chaos of a forced exit. Chaos is what will happen when or if the Supreme Court changes its stance on affirmative action and we have not developed effective exit strategies that will enable equal representation and opportunity in the absence of this initiative.

The significant question becomes: Will institutional leaders and those responsible for managing recruitment, selection, and people processes rise to the challenge? Will they move assertively to develop exit strategies from affirmative action or wait until it is too late?

THE FUTURE

Prescriptions for fixing the ailing affirmative action situation are numerous, contradictory, and often offered shrilly. All of the proposed solutions have one major shortcoming: They continue to focus on how to apply the affirmative action Band-Aid and neglect the key requirement, which is that any adjustments, complements, or alternatives to affirmative action must allow us to obtain the desired racial representation within America's institutions without resorting to race-conscious tools. Prescriptions that fail to do so waste valuable time.

Prescriptions for the Future: Popular Views

Sadly, the prescriptions for change suggested so far have fallen short. They include variations of the following ideas:

- Clarify the benefits of affirmative action in the belief that Americans will be more receptive to the concept if they understand its objectives better.

- Acknowledge the abuses of affirmative action and correct these situations so that affirmative action can command respect from those who are currently unwilling to give it.

- Abolish or minimize affirmative action and rely on the enforcement of antidiscrimination laws.

- Educate people to see others as individuals, not as members of a group.

- Encourage people to become color- and gender-blind.

- Base affirmative action on social class or income, not on race or gender.

The first two suggestions would only tweak the status quo in order to have it continue. As to antidiscrimination laws, if they worked on their own, we would never have had affirmative action in the first place. Injunctions to see people as individuals, or to become color- and gender-blind, will be heeded only by the proverbial choir. To shift focus to social class or income still leaves a system that doesn't work for all people without outside intervention—that is, without the continuing presence of affirmative action in another form.

Prescription for the Future: My View

Affirmative action was created principally because America's institutions weren't ready for diversity. Nearly forty years later, as a society we are no more ready, partly because the affirmative action Band-Aid allowed us to ignore our inability to address diversity effectively.

I can predict with confidence that another forty years of affirmative action will also bring only limited progress. If we are to create communities and organizations that work for diverse populations, we must look beyond affirmative action.

Should we then abolish or minimize affirmative action? No! Until we are able to modify our communities and organizations to work with the realities of diversity, affirmative action will be needed to accommodate diversity, even if that accommodation is to some extent artificial. Remove the Band-Aid, and the policies and practices that are *not* grounded in diversity will naturally become active—and that's not a good outcome.

So, in the short term, we must continue to administer affirmative action. It will not be easy. Going against the grain can be exhausting.

My prescription is to "remodel" organizations and society so that they anticipate and are prepared for all kinds of diversity. To do this, individuals, organizations, and communities must develop a diversity management capability—that is, the ability to make quality decisions in situations that have differences, similarities, and tensions, including those related to race, gender, and ethnicity. An evolving framework for learning and applying this capability is the Strategic Diversity Management craft, which is described in Part 3 in detail.

DEVELOPING A DIVERSITY MANAGEMENT CAPABILITY

If the time for developing alternatives to affirmative action is now, what is our next step? What must leaders do to help their organizations move more broadly toward diversity so that the Band-Aid is no longer needed? In broad stokes, these action steps must be taken:

■ *Affirm your organization's commitment to racial and ethnic representation.* This means working proactively to create and maintain a representative workforce. Without firm evidence of your trustworthy commitment to representation, any effort to exit affirmative action will provoke a defensive reaction to cling to the status quo.

I do mean to stress a *representative* workforce, as opposed to one that is behaviorally diverse. You can commit to representation and also pursue behavioral variations; one idea doesn't preclude the other. But these are two different questions: Do we want representation? Do we want behavioral variations? Although both issues must be examined, representation is the focus of affirmative action.

■ *Work to depoliticize affirmative action within your organization.* If you don't, any serious discussion of affirmative action will continue to take place in the context of political contests. This win–lose environment will hinder progress with any complementary and alternative approaches to affirmative action.

■ *Secure commitment to developing an exit strategy from affirmative action.* The purpose isn't to abandon or oppose affirmative action, but rather to prepare for an orderly transition when the time comes. Affirmative action proponents will accept the concept of an exit strategy only if they are convinced the organization will maintain its will and ability to achieve a representative workforce at all levels.

■ *Legitimize the dialogue.* Developing an effective exit strategy takes creativity and innovation, and those two qualities occur only in an atmosphere of honest debate. As a leader, you must create an environment of trust, openness, and candor. You will be asked, "Why representation?" Your answer should highlight the societal imperative—as opposed to the business rationale—for achieving representation. In many settings, the societal imperative will be greater than any business urgency. Simply state that a democratic and racially and ethnically pluralistic country requires the proportional economic participation and inclusion of all groups.

■ *Develop race-neutral, gender-neutral, and ethnic-neutral people processes for attracting, selecting, and retaining a representa-*

tive workforce. Apply a common set of process criteria and performance standards to all. Do whatever you must to ensure that each criterion and standard is based on absolute requirements and not on personal preferences, conveniences, or traditions.

■ *Build a collective and individual diversity management capability.* Collectively and individually, organizational participants should work to acquire diversity skills (i.e., the ability to recognize, analyze, and respond appropriately to diversity mixtures) and to attain diversity maturity (i.e., the wisdom and judgment necessary for using the skills effectively). These capabilities (described more fully in the chapters in Part 3) are essential to developing an environment that fully engages a representative and behaviorally diverse workforce. Such an environment would greatly facilitate the transition to race-neutral people processes and ultimately make affirmative action unnecessary.

IN CONCLUSION . . .

No individual, indeed no one organization, can "fix" affirmative action or single-handedly teach America how to secure the desired racial representation without resorting to race-conscious tools. But well-informed, well-motivated individuals and organizations working together can make major progress. I urge you, both as an individual and as part of your organization, to become part of the solution to what ails affirmative action and threatens our nation's experiment in diversity, preventing America from becoming all that she can be.

CHAPTER

5

CURRENT STATUS OF THE DIVERSITY FIELD

JUST PLAIN STUCK

MORE THAN A DECADE AGO, I wrote that "the traditional approach to diversity inevitably creates a cycle of crisis, problem recognition, action, great expectations, disappointment, dormancy, and renewed crisis."[1] At the time, I was thinking mostly of managers responsible for implementing affirmative action in their organization. I knew that many of them felt they were going around in circles.

Today, that frustrating affirmative action cycle has morphed into the larger and even more frustrating diversity cycle, but with one major change: There are no longer any great expectations. Corporations and their managers navigate this cycle with purpose and good intentions, but with little—if any—hope of escaping it. Increasingly, people at all levels of their organizations recognize that when it comes to real progress with diversity, they are stuck.

Lately, I keep running into situations that illustrate this "stuckness." Here are four examples:

1. During a presentation to a group that I believed had some experience with diversity management, one audience member stood up and said: "The only reason I am here is that I want to stop the revolving door of minority talent. We can't keep minorities." His company is a large corporation that has earned awards in best practices; it attracts minorities with its reputation but cannot retain them.

His question reflects the latter stages of the affirmative action cycle. It has been asked, in one way or another, for at least twenty years: How do we sustain our progress with "the numbers"?

2.   At a reception, a woman from another major corporation said: "Roosevelt, you know our corporation. In our initial diversity work, we did well with 'the numbers.' Later, we excelled with awareness and relationships. We took a breather and now find that we have lost our hard-won 'numbers.' We're once again in hot pursuit of the numbers, and after this push—I guess—we will go back to awareness. Is this the way it is supposed to work: 'the numbers,' awareness, relax, and then start all over again?"

Her question is a poignant reminder that the cycle is still with us.

3.   The Center for Work-Life Policy launched the Hidden Brain Drain task force to study women and minorities as unrealized assets in the private sector. The task force argues that the professional pipeline is clogged in the United States and the United Kingdom, and that too many highly qualified women and people of color are failing to progress to senior positions. This project's assumptions were grounded firmly in unresolved discussions from the past about remedies for the premature plateauing and glass ceilings experienced by minorities and women. As such, it provides added evidence that the affirmative action cycle has morphed into the "diversity cycle."

4.   A 2004 research report, "Diversity Practices That Work: The American Worker Speaks," sponsored by the National Urban League, found that fewer than one-third (32 percent) of workers thought favorably of diversity programs, while 26 percent were negative about such programs. These findings provide significant evidence of cyclical progress at best.

THE EXPERIENCE OF BEING STUCK

If organizations are stuck, as evidence suggests, what are the dynamics of this situation? What does "being stuck" look like, and what can we do about it?

I am not saying that corporations cannot get off the mark with their diversity efforts or make progress with diversity. Indeed, more than ever, corporations are engaged with diversity efforts. A March

2001 survey by the Society for Human Resource Management (SHRM) and *Fortune* magazine found that responding companies reported involvement in a number of initiatives, as listed in Figure 5-1.

It is noteworthy that company executives reported that these interventions had a positive impact on the bottom line. Their perceptions are shown in Figure 5-2.

F I G U R E 5-1
Diversity initiative involvement.

Initiative	Percentage Responding (n = 87)
Recruiting efforts designed to help increase diversity within the organization	75%
Diversity training initiatives, education, and/or awareness efforts	66%
Community outreach related to diversity	61%
Diversity-related career development (e.g., mentoring)	39%
Celebrating different cultural events (e.g., Black History Month, Hispanic Heritage Month)	38%
Measuring the management of diversity performance of managers	34%
Support groups	24%
Bilingual training for managers and employees	22%
Explicit promotion opportunities to break through the "glass ceiling"	20%
Cultural orientation programs	19%
Training in English as a second language	19%
Use of symbols to promote diversity (e.g., logos or slogans)	17%
Diversity-related conflict resolution	16%
Company-paid literacy training	11%
Very informal efforts, nothing structured at all	19%

SOURCE: "Impact of Diversity Initiatives on the Bottom Line," survey report (Alexandria, VA: SHRM/*Fortune*, 2001), p. 4. Percentages will not equal 100 percent because multiple responses were allowed.

FIGURE 5-2
How diversity initiatives have impacted the bottom line.

Initiative	Percentage Responding (n = 87)
Improves corporate culture	79%
Improves recruitment of new employees	77%
Improves client relations	52%
Higher retention of employees	41%
Decreased complaints and litigation	41%
Enables the organization to move into emerging markets	37%
Positively affects profitability indirectly	32%
Increases productivity	32%
Positively affects profitability	28%
Maximizes brand identity	23%
Has not impacted bottom line	7%
Increased complaints and litigation	1%

SOURCE: "Impact of Diversity Initiatives on the Bottom Line," survey report (Alexandria, VA: SHRM/ *Fortune,* 2001), p. 11. Percentages will not equal 100 percent because multiple responses were allowed.

How, then, are organizations getting stuck? Are they in a rut, like a driver rocking his car back and forth on an icy patch and making *no* progress? No, the survey data suggest that businesses are realizing gains.

Instead, corporations seem to be stuck in a circular route that does not allow them to reach their desired destination. They are like a disoriented driver on a perimeter highway going around and around, covering a great deal of ground but without a clue where to exit. Let's consider an example.

Interstate 285 (I-285) rings the city of Atlanta. In August 1982, Pascual Perez, then a pitcher for the Atlanta Braves baseball team, got on the expressway to go to the Fulton County Stadium for his first start. Unfortunately, he never made it, because he couldn't find the right off-ramp. He circled Atlanta three times and eventually ran out of gas.[2]

I think Perez's experience is analogous to how corporations are stuck with their diversity endeavors. Regardless of what they do, how hard they try, how much energy they expend, they end up running out of gas and are left still asking, "How do we achieve sustainable progress with minorities and women?" And they share many of the same feelings about the unrewarding process.

Exhilaration. Perez must surely have been exhilarated as he was heading to the stadium and his first start with the Atlanta Braves. Similarly, managers often launch their corporation's diversity journey with exhilaration and optimism.

Concern. At some point Perez would have noticed that he had completed his first cycle around the perimeter without finding his exit. An embryonic awareness of being lost must have begun to surface.

Such awareness comes to managers after they have completed a round of diversity activities but sense they have missed the mark—even as stakeholders congratulate them on a job well done. They wonder if they have a complete handle on their responsibilities and if they are losing momentum.

Puzzlement. "What's happening? I've been this way before!" Perez must have been puzzled as he grew certain he had missed his ramp. He may have been disoriented as well, as north, south, east, and west became less certain.

Managers often share the feeling that they have "been this way before" as they launch a second round of diversity activities. They know they have missed the mark with earlier diversity efforts. They have failed to close the revolving doors or dismantle the glass ceilings that hinder advancement for minorities and women. They also realize by now that any progress that was realized will be short-lived. But they, like Perez, are no longer certain of their direction and don't know how to achieve progress that lasts.

Frustration. Imagine Perez's frustration. He realized he was stuck but drove on knowing he wasn't progressing toward his destination. Going forward must have seemed pointless; pulling off for directions would take extra time; quitting was out of the question. None of the options would have seemed promising, yet he was in motion on the expressway. He could only keep going, hoping he might eventually find the right exit.

Managers endure this frustration when they realize their company is quite stuck, even in the midst of multiple activities and good intentions. The company is on the diversity expressway and can show some progress, but the revolving doors and glass ceilings persist. Prototypical here is the manager who exclaims, "We have so many activities going on that I sometimes forget what we are trying to do!" Lots of motion but still stuck. Yet managers hold on to the hope that at some point, the right combination of activities will generate sustainable progress.

Disillusionment. Imagine Perez right before he ran out of gas. He might have wondered if he would ever find the right exit. He went through the motions of driving because no other option made sense. He may have stopped for help, only to be told he had to get back on the expressway. He probably explored a couple of exits that led nowhere. Yet he was committed to making that game. His fans expected it.

Managers reach this point when they find themselves frenetically engaged in activities with no hope of sustainable progress. They can't quit. Both the company and the manager must give the appearance of effort and progress. Neither wants to be caught off the diversity highway. Cynicism grows as their efforts continue. Managers sometimes aim for the illusion of progress until they can surrender the wheel to another driver.

Clearly, managers expend a lot of energy and achieve some short-lived progress while in an I-285 holding pattern. This situation may not seem so bad. If appearances are maintained, organizations can win awards for progress and be lauded as diversity stars. Yet, ultimately, this kind of "being stuck" experience is one of the worst. It allows companies to delude themselves about their lack of genuine progress. Sadly, many companies are in this position today—stuck *and* self-deluded.

WHERE STUCK?

Key to corporate America's inability to move past the point of being stuck is the narrowness of its focus when addressing diversity. This narrowness reveals itself in several ways.

In most organizations, diversity means *workforce* diversity, and workforce diversity means race and gender. As a result, other types of diversity—such as customer, product, function, acquisition/merger, family, or community diversity—go unaddressed.

The undue emphasis on workforce diversity creates a focus on two questions:

1. How do we create a more diverse workforce with respect to race and gender?

2. How do we ensure harmony among workforce participants?

So entrenched is this focus that to deemphasize these questions is to abandon the crux of diversity work. As a result, the organization's diversity progress is erroneously measured "by the numbers" and by indicators of harmony.

The preoccupation with race and gender leads managers to think that the elimination of racism, sexism, and prejudices in general will ensure diversity success. This belief, which is now hardened into dogma, often blinds them to other equally formidable barriers to diversity success.

In seeking to create diversity-capable companies with respect to "numbers" and relationships, for example, organizational leaders have tended to view diversity management as a managerial tool and have scheduled training accordingly. They have essentially ignored skills training that would allow individual contributors to convert diversity management into a personal tool for addressing issues important to them.

Why does this matter? Because it encourages rank-and-file associates to remain unengaged, believing diversity management is something that applies just to the boss. Since leaders in many corporations are primarily white men, minorities and women may see diversity training as irrelevant to themselves. The implications are clear. Unless diversity management becomes personally valuable to individual contributors, its chances of becoming embedded in organization and communities are nil.

The excessive focus on workforce diversity creates another impediment to diversity progress. Companies that have worked exclusively on workforce diversity have little notion about how to expand their efforts. They are justifiably dubious, given their narrow experience, that the politicized efforts related to "people" diversity will work for "nonpeople" dimensions, and their imaginations have taken them no further.

Unable to make the connections, they resist conversations about diversity in general, fearing that they will dilute attention from their particular interest area. In doing so, they miss out on approaches that could apply to *all* diversity dimensions (e.g., customers, products, functions) and that also could be useful in their silo diversity effort. Again, the error is self-perpetuating. Practitioners are stuck on the silo approach, which, in turn, keeps them reenacting the I-285 experience.

Also contributing to diversity "stuckness" is the insistence on making the business case for workforce diversity. Diversity conferences are replete with formal and informal presentations on this topic. Diversity managers seem convinced that making this case will "really" convince their senior management of the importance of achieving and maintaining workforce diversity. Once that happens, they believe, sustainable advancement will follow.

It is true that achieving and maintaining workforce diversity benefits both companies and society. However, applying appropriate diversity concepts and techniques to other mixtures—such as globalism, innovation, multiple products, multiple brands, functional units, and departments—will more likely enhance corporate profits in a way that senior management can perceive.

Exaggerating the bottom-line potential of people diversity and ignoring the bottom-line benefits of nonpeople diversity initiatives leads to a number of wrong off-ramps. Chief among them is a murky understanding of what workforce diversity interventions have the potential to achieve and how managers can assess their success. Also important is the failure to demonstrate the powerful financial benefits of diversity interventions when applied to nonpeople strategic issues.

WHY STUCK?

Several factors keep diversity managers stuck. Let's identify and explain some of them.

■   *Workforce diversity initiatives have been politicized from their inception.* Thinkers on diversity issues historically have viewed these initiatives as an extension or outgrowth of the Civil Rights Movement. As a result, diversity practitioners have focused on *racial* diversity, perceived diversity as a legal and moral matter, presumed the existence of a victim and a victimizer, and identified racism as the major barrier to diversity success.

Writing about the civil rights vision, Thomas Sowell notes two related characteristics:

> One of the most central—and most controversial—premises of the civil rights vision is that statistically significant disparities in incomes, occupations, education, etc. represent moral inequities and are caused by "society." Another central premise of the civil rights vision is that belief in innate inferiority explains policies and practices of differential treatment, whether expressed in overt hostility or in institutional policies or individual decisions that result in statistical disparities.[3]

Diversity managers have tended to focus almost exclusively on the "isms" as the barrier to diversity success. From this perspective, it is all but impossible to entertain diversity issues *not* grounded in racism or any other "isms." It may be true that different forms of prejudice constitute major barriers to diversity progress, but other factors are important, too. To assume that disparities suggest the presence of prejudice on the basis of race or sex or other attribute can lead to misdiagnoses and hence poor problem solving. These stubborn errors keep organizations circling the diversity equivalent of the I-285 expressway.

■ *Diversity managers are uncomfortable with diversity tensions.* They presume that if racism or sexism or other "isms" are eliminated, there will be no tensions. When tensions persist in spite of their efforts, they feel they have failed and should try again. In reality, however, tensions will *always* persist. With diversity comes diversity tension. Getting past "stuck" requires a willingness to accept this reality and an ability to make quality decisions in spite of the existence of tensions.

■ *Diversity advocates often believe that progress with desegregation has been inadequate.* A focus on the "isms" and discomfort with diversity tension are not the only aspects of the link between the Civil Rights Movement and diversity initiatives that keep people circling the highway. In 2004, fifty years after the original court decision, discussions about the benefits of *Brown* v. *Board of Education of Topeka* made clear that many supporters of the Civil Rights Movement believe that more could and should be done with respect to racial desegregation. One school of thought still questions the merits of the government's strategy and notes that although segregation in schools has been made illegal, most public school students still experience segregated learning.[4]

For those who see limited progress with racial desegregation, getting stuck in the I-285 circle is not the worst thing that could happen to a corporation. As they see it, the fact that the organization is still circling means it is still engaged in the civil rights cause. That not only puts them on the side of the angels; it serves the corporation's image as well. This is true even if these managers know they are hopelessly going in circles.

■ *Even a "stuck" corporation can do quality work in the diversity field.* This is a critical point. I-285 is roughly sixty-two miles long.

Even though he was frustrated, Perez could still have experienced a measure of enjoyment on his way to the game. He might, for example, have watched airplanes land and take off at the Hartsfield-Jackson Atlanta International Airport, stopped for a meal at any of a number of quality restaurants, and viewed historic, interesting communities. But he still would have been lost.

Analogous is the good diversity work of the stuck corporation. A company can do quality work—even pioneering work—on diversity programs that focus on "the numbers" and working relationships but remain stuck, unable to maintain its hard-won gains without a constant recycling.

This predicament can be heart wrenching. Managers in such companies see that the work is good and dare to hope that it will be lasting. They move through an emotional cycle in concert with their diversity cycle, spiraling repeatedly from joy and hope—"Maybe we're not stuck!"—into profound frustration when reality hits. What is worse, their company is still stuck, only now the glass ceilings and revolving doors are more entrenched.

■ *Society rewards effort with diversity, thus encouraging cynicism.* Society often doesn't distinguish between a company's efforts and its achievement. Society awards corporations that persevere with diversity efforts even while stuck. This encourages cynicism in some companies, leaving them willing to stay in an I-285 holding pattern.

Senior managers in these companies settle for projecting an image that minimizes chances of a public relations disaster or successful litigation against them. Diversity initiatives are used as a protective fence. They vigorously campaign for "best practices" awards without trying to address issues that have hamstrung them for some time. This strategy may work in the short term, but it has a high cost: lack of trust. Employees will recognize this as deception and may deeply distrust senior management.

One manager, caught in a best practices campaign, said: "I know this is only window dressing, but our senior executives want us on the list. Hopefully, we can make some real progress after winning recognition." That's unlikely. The mystified rank-and-file workers

may wonder, "How did we win this award? I don't understand!" Their
sense of distrust increases and jeopardizes real progress. Without the
active participation of employees, no diversity initiative can succeed.

■   *Corporations emulate companies that are stuck.* They do this
through benchmarking, a common practice in the diversity field. At a
variety of conferences and through research projects, diversity managers search for insights and practices to inform the work of their
corporations. The best candidates for benchmarking are organizations that have been designated "diversity best practices" enterprises.
If these award-winning companies are stuck (and many are), then
benchmarking managers are emulating the efforts of the "stuck." So
the I-285 diversity experience becomes the model.

■   *Many leaders believe that no new solutions are needed.* All
that is necessary, they think, is the will to act. The unfortunate consequence has been a reluctance to invest in research and development
in diversity and diversity management. These leaders look for best
practices as a way to activate the will of their organizations, as opposed to looking for solutions that are substantively different. Inadequate R&D is a major contributing factor to being stuck.

■   *Some senior executives think being stuck is the "state of the
art."* They know that they are stuck, but they believe that any company seriously engaged with diversity will remain stuck until the
"state of the art" advances. They are content to stay in the holding
pattern as long as others are there, too. These leaders seek to run with
the pack. If the pack advances, they move too. If not, they circle
contentedly, waiting for others to lead.

■   *Many leaders are reluctant to admit that they need help.*
Some leaders know that they are stuck but think they can find the
appropriate exit on their own if they just try hard enough. They are
like the proverbial husband at the wheel of his car who knows he is
lost but refuses help, as if accepting it will damage his credibility.
   Organizational leaders may also refuse to admit that they need
help, believing that it signals a lack of commitment or an inability to
meet their diversity performance objectives. So they persevere in

good faith, believing that they are at least doing the "right thing." They hope against hope that "this time around" they'll have a real breakthrough to sustainable progress. These leaders, unlike cynical ones, do expect and hope to see real progress if they try long and hard enough. Their insistence on going it alone, however, can cost their organizations considerable time and money.

Other leaders are reluctant to discuss diversity challenges for fear others will think that their organizations are vulnerable to lawsuits or public relations embarrassments or, worse still, that they are not doing their job. As a result, diversity is an area where leaders resist talking about their challenges until a full-blown crisis appears.

A few years ago, senior executives from several large, reputable companies met to discuss their difficulties in increasing the presence of minorities within their organizations. Yet after a brief discussion of these challenges, they shifted the conversation to the more familiar, less threatening ground of best practices and benchmarking.

This seemed odd. The meeting had been called to examine the problems that companies were having. By their presence, participants implicitly admitted that they didn't have the answers. Yet they comforted themselves by sharing diversity remedies that had created so little progress it was necessary to get together to examine problems. Their time would have been better spent in analysis and problem solving rather than benchmarking ineffective "solutions."

■   *Vagueness reigns.* Here, leaders talk about the importance and potential benefits of diversity, but few are specific about the desired state and the challenges implicit in attaining their goal. Even when diversity champions know, for example, that they want to increase the presence of minorities and women, they often shy away from specifics to avoid the appearance of quotas. They gloss over the challenges as well.

As a result, these leaders often cite vague objectives and murky definitions of success, making it nearly impossible to measure or celebrate progress. In such an environment, a fire-fighting, crisis-driven approach can emerge. Strategic, proactive effort is difficult when leaders avoid candid conversations while simultaneously repeating mottoes such as "We celebrate diversity."

Even when managers are passionate and committed, if objectives are ill defined, organizations are unlikely to achieve diversity success. It's hard to get off the expressway at the right place if you don't know where you're going.

■   *Conceptual and process confusion reigns.* Another reason diversity objectives stay unclear is that a variety of concepts are viewed as synonymous. Terms such as *diversity, diversity management, equal opportunity, affirmative action, desegregation, integration, pluralism,* and *multiculturalism* are used interchangeably as if there were no difference. It is as if Perez, stuck on 1-285, decided any old exit would do.

Yet it is not true, as one executive in a major corporation told his colleagues, that diversity can be defined in any number of ways. "What matters," he proclaimed, "is how *we* define it." That outlook is self-defeating. Managers may choose their diversity focus, but the nature of diversity remains the same.

Managers who don't differentiate among approaches or processes also contribute to today's "stuckness." One senior in-house manager told me, "All diversity approaches are the same. It does not matter which you use." Another manager revealed a plan where only the language had been changed to turn an affirmative action strategy into a diversity roadmap. When asked how the two plans differed, he declined to comment.

Confusion such as this means that many maps of the diversity expressway are unreliable at best and useless at worst. They contribute to the likelihood of staying stuck.

■   *Managers have difficulty subscribing simultaneously to two or more approaches.* As a result, they tend to adopt an either/or mindset toward approach alternatives, or to deny that significant differences can exist among them. When a corporation's leaders subscribe to this view, they shut down the exploration of new approaches and encourage status quo thinking. In short, this perspective works to lock in current practices and makes it difficult to escape being stuck.

ANTIDOTE FOR BEING STUCK

The condition of "stuckness" is in danger of becoming entrenched, draining the discipline of diversity of its vitality and immobilizing its leaders. But this doesn't need to happen. Diversity champions can find their way off the I-285 expressway and reach their destination, but doing so will require innovation and discipline.

To become unstuck, corporations and their leaders must meet several conditions. They must adopt a new frame of reference that embraces these concepts:

Multiple Perspectives. Individuals and corporations must learn to use at least two perspectives—Civil Rights Movement and at least one other—simultaneously. They need not abandon the traditional perspective of the Civil Rights Movement, but they must be willing to complement or supplement it.

An Alternative Framework. Society and corporations will then need a decision-making framework grounded in the other perspective. This framework will provide a formal structure for the alternative approach that would complement or supplement the traditional civil rights approach.

Capability Versus Solution. The alternative framework should empower and equip leaders to develop their own answers, rather than equip them with ready-made "solutions." As with any craft, mastery would require practice.

Universality. The alternative framework must be universal in its application, so it can be used beyond workforce and even workplace mixtures to those associated with the community and home. Stated differently, this universality of application will allow managers to move beyond silo approaches to diversity. "One approach, multiple applications" is the goal.

Accommodation of Diversity Tension. Diversity champions will need decision-making frameworks that accommodate the reality of diversity tension. Both individuals and organizations will have to be effective in the midst of continuing tension.

Multiple Causation. Effectiveness at the next level of diversity management will require acknowledging that although sexism, racism, and other "isms" may be causes of poor decision making in the midst of diversity, factors such as complexity and cognitive limitations can hinder diversity progress, too.

A Focus on Individuals, as well as Organizations and Managers. To get off the diversity expressway, diversity managers, theorists, and champions have to make diversity management relevant not only for organizations and their leaders but for their rank-and-file members as well. Frameworks must allow for application at home and in the community as well as in the workplace.

Ownership. Individuals (e.g., associates, managers, executives, *and* diversity leaders) will have to own the "next level" framework and perspective. More than buy-in will be required. That is, individuals cannot simply endorse the "next level" tools. They must include them in their personal tool kit and use them in their decision making regarding diversity issues, whether in the workplace, the home, or the community. Visible ownership will be a key to success.

Quality Maps. Frameworks that clearly delineate concepts, principles, and skills will be needed. These structures should be grounded in solid research that may draw from benchmark efforts but must go beyond them.

IN CONCLUSION . . .

I believe that Strategic Diversity Management (SDM) can serve as the framework bridge that organizations, leaders, and rank-and-file employees use to reach the next level of diversity management. SDM possesses or fosters the attributes that companies and their diversity leaders need if they are to become unstuck.

First, though, let me explain how my own experiences and personal odyssey brought me to this stage in my thinking.

CHAPTER

A PERSONAL ODYSSEY

ANY TIME YOU SET OUT on a complex journey, it helps to be
very clear about your starting point. Those who are eager to move to
the next level with diversity will find it valuable, probably even essential, to clarify who they are in this respect and what they currently
believe about the topic.

This statement may strike you as completely self-evident, and yet
as I travel around the country talking about diversity issues, I find that
very often people are not quite clear about what they hold dear in
this area, even when they speak with passion. Another common reaction: a self-righteous attitude.

More so than you might expect, then, an objective, fully candid
introspection is a necessary building block for thinking about the next
level.

I'll start with myself.

In this chapter I summarize my own experiences with diversity,
describing how my views have evolved over the years. I offer them
for two reasons. One, I wish to give you a context for understanding
the "next level" prescriptions offered in the next section of this book
and the terminology used. Two, I hope my experience will encourage
you to do your own introspection. Toward that end, this chapter concludes with some questions to guide you.

1970S: DIVERSITY EQUALS DIFFERENCES BETWEEN FUNCTIONS

In the early seventies, I was a doctoral student at the Harvard Business School. It was here, while studying with two professors, Paul R. Lawrence and Jay Lorsch, that I encountered my first serious discussion of diversity. However, it focused not on race and gender or the workforce, but on diversity between functions.

Lawrence and Lorsch were looking for a way to ensure that the different functions in a corporation were differentiated enough to achieve their assigned tasks while simultaneously being part of an integrated whole. The managerial or "managing diversity" challenge was to design organizations that achieved the appropriate amounts of differentiation and integration.[1]

In two respects, Lawrence and Lorsch's views differed from those I would later espouse. First, they equated diversity solely with differences. Second, their thinking represented a silo approach to diversity—one focused on differences among functional units in the company, not differences in general or a universal perspective. In one respect, however, they saw differences (diversity) as I would later perceive them—as inherently neither good nor bad.

As a student, I thought fleetingly that the dynamics of differentiation and integration could also be applied to race relations. At the time, however, I wasn't focused on race relations, and so I did not pursue this line of thinking.

Nonetheless, my early exposure to the professors' framework had a significant impact. Because they were concerned with functional units, workforce diversity did not then, and does not now, come immediately to mind when I hear the word *diversity*.

My doctoral work also greatly influenced my professional direction. From my research experiences, I knew that relatively little work had been conducted about diversity in organizations. So, some ten years later, I decided that my role with respect to diversity would be primarily as a researcher and not as an advocate. That decision led me to write several works and, ultimately, to found the American Institute for Managing Diversity (AIMD).

1984–1995: DIVERSITY EQUALS WORKFORCE DIFFERENCES

I founded the AIMD in 1984, primarily because I thought a different perspective on racial issues within the workforce was needed. At the time, corporate executives were struggling to sustain achievements in affirmative action that had improved the representation of minorities in their workforce. I believed that they needed something more than simple representation—they needed an effective complement to affirmative action. I also believed that AIMD could help create this complement, both by conducting research and facilitating managed change. Finally, I saw Lawrence and Lorsch's framework of differentiation and integration as a possible point of departure.

In one of my first published articles on diversity, "From Affirmative Action to Affirming Diversity," I argued for complementing affirmative action with something called "managing diversity." Although I did not specifically define diversity in the article, I did have racial, ethnic, and gender differences in mind. On the other hand, I was much more deliberate about defining what it means to manage diversity. I wrote: "Managing diversity does not mean controlling or containing diversity, it means enabling every member of your workforce to perform to his or her potential."[2] I emphasized "managing" because I believed that managing a diverse workforce might be different from managing a homogeneous one.

The next year, I published my first book-length work: *Beyond Race and Gender: Unleashing the Power of Your Total Workforce by Managing Diversity*. In it, I expanded my definition of diversity:

> Diversity includes everyone; it is not something that is defined by race or gender. It extends to age, personal and corporate background, education, function, and personality. It includes life-style, sexual preference, geographic origin, tenure with the organization, exempt or nonexempt status, and management or non-management [experience]. . . . In this expanded context, white males are as diverse as their colleagues. A commitment to diversity is a commitment to all employees, not an attempt at preferential treatment.[3]

I also refined my definition of managing diversity as a "comprehensive managerial process for developing an environment that works for all employees."

The goal of this process was to empower corporations to develop a natural capability for tapping the potential of all employees. "Natural" meant that this capability became a part of the organization's essence, rather than something that went against the grain. Under this definition, tapping the potential of all employees becomes part and parcel of doing business. This was critical because it was the lack of a natural capability to manage diversity that created the need for affirmative action in the first place (and makes exiting from affirmative action so difficult today).

During this period, I talked about all types of workforce differences, yet inevitably the conversation always returned to race and gender. It wasn't that I didn't want to talk about race and gender. Instead, I was frustrated at not being able to explore how broadly the concept of diversity could be applied. However, this intention was not always understood. It was during the late eighties and early nineties that I first encountered tension between my notion of managing diversity and the proponents of the Civil Rights Movement and affirmative action. They believed that I wanted to abandon affirmative action. Although I favored affirmative action and did not want to see it abandoned, this perception persists for some people to this day.

Finally, during this period, the term *managing diversity* became politicized. It became code for affirmative action and equal opportunity, and thus became part of the public debate about policy. Politicization has greatly hindered the acceptance and further development of the concept. Once it set in, substantive discussion about managing diversity as I defined it became more difficult.

1995–2000: DIVERSITY EQUALS *ANY* DIFFERENCES AND SIMILARITIES

In the mid-1990s, new complaints surfaced. Critics pointed out that whereas I claimed that diversity was broader than race and gender, my examples still focused on race and gender workforce issues.

I took this criticism to heart. Yet, as I prepared to address broader diversity issues, I hit a roadblock. My personal definitions were inadequate to the task. My concept of diversity centered on differences in the *workforce,* and my definition for managing diversity really was about managing workforce diversity and was not easily adaptable beyond it. Moving beyond the workforce required new definitional tools.

I set about rethinking my definitions, and in 1996, in a new book (*Redefining Diversity*), I proposed this idea:

> Diversity refers to *any* mixture of items characterized by differences and similarities.[4]

Speaking of "any mixture" reflected my desire for a definition that could be applied wherever needed. "Differences and similarities" was a departure from the traditional practice of focusing only on differences. The expanded definition seemed appropriate when moving beyond the workforce. It also communicated my maturing understanding of diversity.

In the same book, I also broadened my definition of "diversity management" as a process for addressing *any* diversity mixture, to distinguish it from the process of "managing workforce diversity." I developed eight action options that could be used with *any* diversity mixture. These actions were in response to the question, "Exactly what do you do when you manage diversity?" To demonstrate the application of the ideas, I looked at diversity with respect to people, lifestyles, functions, globalism, and management approaches.[5]

I also wanted to show that diversity management could be used by managers *and* rank-and-file employees. This was a change from earlier thinking, where I suggested that creating environments that empowered all associates was the job of management.

I felt a sense of accomplishment. I had developed a set of definitions that could be used with all kinds of diversity mixtures. I had also developed a framework that specified the responses that people could use when making decisions about diversity. Still, *Redefining Diversity* looked only at workplace and organizational issues. I had not positioned diversity management to be useful in addressing personal concerns. Work remained to be done.

Not everyone appreciated the book. Critics of diversity management argued that it was not practical and did not deal with the "meat and potatoes" issues of race and gender in the workforce. They neither understood nor accepted that diversity management was a capability that could be used wherever doing so was advantageous—including where the concerns were about race and gender.

Thus, three years later I wrote another book—*Building a House for Diversity*—that explored further the notion that individuals could learn to respond effectively to the diversity mixtures they were bound to encounter in all aspects of their lives, both at work and outside it. In this book, I made clear the skills and maturity that are needed to use the diversity framework successfully. I also became very aware that diversity management as a universal capability required considerable practice. Finally, I tried to expand the discussion from "What should my manager or organization be doing about diversity?" to "What should *I* be doing about diversity?"

This shift has been difficult. Traditional approaches place the onus for effective diversity management on managers. *Building a House for Diversity* argues that individuals also have a personal responsibility to manage diversity effectively. In fact, unless they do so, the organization as a whole cannot be effective with diversity.[6]

This perspective has many advantages. Most important, it reflects the reality of diversity efforts. It is also more democratic and less paternalistic than earlier perspectives, and therefore more personal. As a result, it is considerably more meaningful to groups, particularly minorities and women, who saw little personal applicability to earlier diversity efforts.

Building a House for Diversity represented substantial progress toward completing my theoretical journey. Using Lawrence and Lorsch's work as a departure point, I had evolved a framework that addressed diversity as "any mixture characterized by differences, similarities, and related tensions" and could be used by executives, managers, and individual contributors. I was pleased with this progress.

2000 AND FORWARD: TOWARD USER-FRIENDLINESS

Having made substantial progress in my theoretical journey, I have focused recently on making the approach user-friendly. In this regard, two refinements were essential.

First, to communicate my thinking more clearly, I stressed what diversity is and what it is not. Diversity is the *differences* and *similarities* that exist among the elements of a specific mixture. It does not refer solely to differentiating characteristics, nor to characteristics that are easily observable. Diversity is both dynamic and interactive. It cannot be predicted from external appearances.

This definition can be difficult to understand. In practice, managers who want a "diverse workforce" often focus on the individual and not his or her diversity. One manager seeking a racially and ethnically diverse work team recruited qualified representatives of ten racial and ethnic groups and pronounced his company more diverse. To a certain extent, he is correct. He has created a representative team of different races and ethnicities. But he has no idea *how* diverse the team is. The new recruits *may* be diverse only in race and ethnicity. Or they *could* be different and similar along any number of dimensions in ways that might (or might not) be compatible. They could, for example, differ in work experience, age, gender, religion, personality, geographic origins, or a variety of other variables. The manager simply doesn't know.

To know the extent to which people are different and similar, the manager must dig further. Those who are willing to do so can create a workforce that is both representative and diverse. Furthermore, they can decide first what kind of diversity they do and do not want, and then seek individuals whose characteristics and interactions will create this diversity.

Second, I redefined diversity management to focus on "strategic" mixtures and quality decision making. I now use the term *Strategic Diversity Management*, which I define as "the craft of making quality decisions in the midst of strategic (critical) differences, similarities, and tensions."

This definition acknowledges that no company or person can, or even should, address *all* diversity mixtures—only the ones that are strategic (i.e., critical to achieving a mission or vision). Once identified as strategic, however, any mixture can be addressed. Take note: I mean this definition to include mission and vision of *both* the organization and the individuals within it.

In sum, the framework that I began constructing twenty-one years ago with a focus on diversity of functions and lines of business has gradually evolved to one that can be used universally with any kind of diversity (see Figure 6-1). I hope this modified framework will be more accessible so that it can be extended beyond the workplace into communities, nonbusiness enterprises, and families. Indeed, over the past few years, I have seen it used in a wide variety of organizational and community settings. I find this encouraging.

A CRAFT FOR CHANGE

If the craft of Strategic Diversity Management can be applied to all kinds of diversity, then, of course, that includes the traditional areas of race and gender. Because diversity programs are so identified with race, there is a common tendency to assume that Strategic Diversity Management must have somehow developed within the context of the Civil Rights Movement. Not so.

SDM, as I define it, did not evolve as part of the legacy of the civil rights movement, but rather as part of a broader attempt to deal with differences and similarities among organizational units, starting all the way back with my Harvard professors in the 1970s.

That is one of the reasons I have tracked the evolution of SDM in this chapter—to counter the widespread confusion on this point. This is not to say, however, that Strategic Diversity Management and the civil rights movement are wholly unrelated. There are critical differences and similarities between them, and, more to point, SDM can be used to support achievement of the movement's agenda.

SDM, in fact, offers a powerful tool to address some of our most vexing societal tensions, including those commonly referred to today

FIGURE 6-1
Evolution of my personal thoughts.

Time Period	Diversity Definition	Process Definition	Silo or Universal?	Actor(s)?
Doctoral Program 1970s	Diversity equals functional differences.	Design organization so that appropriate differentiation and integration will be achieved.	Silo (functional diversity)	Managers
Early Years at AIMD 1984–1995	Diversity equals all workforce differences, plus a hint about differences beyond the workforce.	Managing workforce diversity meant developing an environment that works for all employees.	Silo (workforce diversity)	Managers
Middle Years at AIMD 1996–2000	Diversity refers to any mixture of items characterized by differences and similarities.	Diversity management meant using the eight diversity action options to respond to any diversity mixture.	Universal (any diversity mixture)	Managers and individual contributors/ community leaders and members
Most Recent Years at AIMD 2001–2005	Diversity refers to the mixture of differences, similarities, and tensions that can exist among the elements of a pluralistic mixture.	Diversity management became "Strategic Diversity Management (SDM)," defined as the craft of making quality decisions amid differences, similarities, and tensions.	Universal (any set of differences, similarities, and tensions in the workplace, community, home, or wherever)	Managers and individual contributors/ community leaders and members

as "cultural wars," such as conflicts over religion, immigration, school prayer, abortion, and gay marriage.

Earlier chapters looked at the relationship between SDM and these larger issues. The next section will explore SDM in detail. Although most of the applications discussed will be in a business environment, I urge you to keep in mind its potential in other contexts.

A TASK FOR READERS

My goal in tracing the evolution of my thinking about diversity was largely to encourage you to explore your own unique perspective. Flushing out this perspective will take effort, but the rewards are worth it. In the short term, your self-knowledge will make you better prepared to immerse yourself in this book and to fully explore its ideas. In the longer term, it will help you to address diversity in all its forms with wisdom and purpose.

The questions that follow should help you get started. I urge you not to skip these questions and to think deeply about your responses. There are no right or wrong answers. What's important is that they be honest ones.

Exploring Your Perspective on Diversity

1. How do I define diversity?

2. Do I know how I "cope with" the diversity that matters to me?

3. Do I know how my organization defines and addresses diversity?

4. Am I comfortable with my organization's view and handling of diversity?

5. Am I content with my own definition and managing of diversity?

6. Does my personal definition of diversity help me to know how to approach diversity-related issues?

7. How could my framework be more useful?

8. Where might it help to complement my current diversity definition and efforts with another one?

9. How—if at all—have my definitions of and framework for diversity changed over the last five years?

10. Am I open to learning about and trying out new definitions of and processes to address diversity?

PART THREE

THE CRAFT OF STRATEGIC DIVERSITY MANAGEMENT

STRATEGIC DIVERSITY MANAGEMENT

UNDERGIRDING CONCEPTS

DIVERSITY IS NOT AN ABSTRACT CONCEPT; it is made tangible every day, in every organization, wherever two or more people are engaged in a common activity. And, like anything else that involves human beings, it can be frustratingly complex. One tried-and-true way to accommodate complexity is to overlay it with concepts and an organized methodology that provide a roadmap for navigating the unexpected. It is in this spirit that I invite you to explore Strategic Diversity Management (SDM).

SDM is, at its core, a craft that enhances decision making. I believe that, properly understood and used, it can serve as a bridge to the next level with diversity.

In this chapter, I introduce the five basic concepts that undergird SDM. Then Chapter 8 explores the fundamentals that evolve from these concepts. Chapter 9 details the Strategic Diversity Management Process (SDMP), a tool that can facilitate mastery of the craft. Chapter 10 describes two essential capabilities—diversity skills and diversity maturity—that are honed by practice. Finally, Chapter 11 offers tips for novices aspiring to master the SDM craft.

CONCEPT 1: DIVERSITY—WHAT IT IS, WHAT IT ISN'T

You will recall that I define diversity as "the mix of differences, similarities, and tensions that can exist among the elements of a collective mixture."

How do we know if a mixture is diverse? We can't tell just by looking at people. We must first specify which dimensions we're interested in, which ones we consider significant. Are we concerned about race, gender, ethnicity, or geographic origin? Perhaps we have decided that the critical element is age, political affiliation, socioeconomic class, or sexual orientation, or maybe some combination of those factors. For each significant dimension, the first core question would be: How different or similar are the members of the mixture?

It could be that on the designated significant dimensions of age, tenure with organization, and educational background, everyone in the group differs from everyone else, which probably is not good news. Potentially, this could be a very fragmented, even chaotic group. The group's manager and its members would need extensive diversity management skills to be effective in such a situation.

Alternatively, members of the group may be similar on all of these significant dimensions. Such a homogenous group might lack sufficient diversity to be optimally effective.

Another possibility is a group where there are similarities and differences among people on these critical dimensions. We would say that, as far as these specific dimensions are concerned, this is a diverse group.

Obviously, some groups are homogeneous on one dimension, fragmented or chaotic on another, and diverse on still another. A group of ten white males, for example, could differ from each other as to why they accepted employment with an enterprise and with respect to what they expect from the organization. On the other hand, these same ten individuals could be the same in regard to race, gender, age, and religion, while being similar or different along the dimensions of skill, marital status, and geographic origin. What's important here is to understand that we can't specify how diverse a group is until we indicate the dimension in question.

In practice, in the United States, when someone says, "This is a diverse group," most often the unstated reference is to race, ethnicity, or gender. And particularly in the workplace, diversity is often understood to mean affirmative action, with a focus on race and gender. This circumstance profoundly shortchanges the reality of diversity.

When defined accurately, diversity is a universal phenomenon. That means that we can apply techniques for its management to *any* set of differences, similarities, and tensions in the midst of *any* collective mixture. It is precisely the recognition of a universal scope that gives SDM the potential to add value and increase effectiveness in addressing any diverse mixture.

CONCEPT 2: STRATEGIC DIVERSITY MANAGEMENT IS A LEARNABLE CRAFT

Strategic Diversity Management is a craft for enhancing the way people make quality decisions in situations where there are critical differences, similarities, and tensions. Because it is a cognitive craft, anyone can *learn* to use it.

This fact is crucial. Everyone can use the framework effectively. It matters not whether a person has a "good heart" or an unpleasant attitude. It doesn't matter if someone is afflicted with the "isms" (e.g., racism, sexism, ageism) or free of them. What matters is this: Can this person make quality decisions? Successful use of SDM does not depend on the vague concepts of personal attributes or characteristics. It requires the ability to think and act in certain ways, and that is what ensures that it is doable. Three key questions surface immediately from this definition:

1. *What is a quality decision?* A quality decision is one that helps people and organizations accomplish three important goals: mission (what are we seeking to do?), vision (what would success look like ideally?), and strategy (how will we gain maximum competitive standing?).

A decision that does not maximize progress toward those three things is not a quality one. By implication, those who wish to make quality decisions in the midst of diversity, managers included, must take the time to know and understand their own and their organization's mission, vision, and strategy. Furthermore, it's important to recognize here that managers and individual contributors need to maintain a dual perspective, simultaneously attending to their own mission, vision, and strategy *and* that of the organization.

2.   *What constitutes a critical set of differences, similarities, and tensions?* Other ways to ask this question are: How do I decide what diversity to address? How do I avoid being overwhelmed by all the different types of diversity that might beckon my attention?

The value of the universal definition of diversity is its prescription that you take a strategic approach. You decide which diversity to address by identifying the one you *must* address if you are to achieve your goals in a way that is consistent with agreed-on strategy. Ask yourself: What diversity really matters if you and your organization are to achieve your goals, and what can you afford to ignore? For example, an organization's leadership may decide that diversity with respect to skill and ability to travel is critical for their business and then set out to satisfy this need. Simultaneously, they may specify that they cannot have diversity on the dimensions of "commitment to safety" and "ability to accept responsibility." On all other dimensions, however, they conclude that they have no diversity requirements. So, for instance, the leadership would be receptive if all new recruits possessed the same religious beliefs or differed widely.

The obvious implication is that, depending on the situation, you may need either a broad or a narrow perspective. You may decide that you must address several dimensions of diversity to achieve the desired goals. Sometimes you may need to address only one. You won't really know until you examine the situation.

Fairly often, when people first hear these universal definitions, they complain, "You are defining the SDM craft so broadly that its concepts have no meaning." A more accurate observation would be, "By defining this craft's parameters strategically, you put the burden of analysis on me." And that is absolutely my intent. Those who strive for simple definitions do so at the expense of effectiveness.

3.   *Where could we use SDM?* The craft can be used in many places and with many issues, wherever a blend of differences, similarities, and tensions exists.

In the workplace, SDM can be applied to issues having to do with:

- Functions
- Acquisitions and mergers
- Workforce composition
- Teams
- Product lines
- Customers and markets

At home, it works with issues having to do with:

- Blended families

- Generations

- Political preferences

- Spouses

In the community and the larger society, SDM is applicable to issues having to do with:

- Immigration

- Cultural wars

- Race, ethnicity, gender

- Religion

- Public school systems

CONCEPT 3: DIVERSITY TENSION IS NATURAL

Diversity tension is the stress, strain, and anxiety that tend to flow from the interaction of differences and similarities. It is *not* automatic conflict or hostility. It is, in fact, a natural accompaniment of diversity. This is important to remember when assessing diversity progress. Frequently, diversity tension is seen as a sign of a lack of progress when that is not necessarily so.

In Atlanta, where we have considerable racial diversity, I recently heard this comment: "One of my problems with Atlanta is that everything is black and white; everything boils down to race. If you scrub the surface a little, you always encounter racial tension." My response is that you will always have racial tension where you have racial diversity. The goal is not to eliminate tension, but rather to make quality decisions in spite of it.

Can we have racial harmony and racial tension simultaneously? Of course. Multiple races can achieve harmony around a shared mission, vision, and strategy, and they can make quality decisions in the midst of their racial diversity. Yet even in this situation, racial tension can exist.

Why is diversity tension a "given"? I think it has to do with the capacity of humans to deal with differences. While some of us do better than others, for all of us, some types of differences present significant challenges. Indeed, research suggests that when humans experience a threat to their self-esteem, they respond by becoming angry with someone who is of a different social group, sex, or ethnicity. Some researchers even hypothesize that at a very basic level, people are wired to distrust outsiders. Nancy Wartik, a commentator on health issues, writes in *The New York Times* that "prejudice may have evolutionary roots, having developed as a quick, crude way for early humans to protect themselves from danger."[1] In reality, caution when encountering someone we don't know can be both prejudicial and, at the same time, a prudent, self-defensive practice.

Those who don't understand or appreciate diversity tension can reach erroneous conclusions. Consider the case of an African-American who became his company's first senior executive of color. Many times, support personnel challenged him, as if he didn't really have an office in the building. Once a security guard accompanied him from the lobby upstairs to the corporate suite, to make certain that he did have an office there.

The executive interprets these actions as indicators of racism, lack of good intention on the organization's part, and evidence of how far the corporation has to go with diversity. He remains closed to other possibilities. His response, although certainly understandable, is not helpful.

At this junction you may be thinking, "Roosevelt, come on! What else can this be but a case of racism?" The reality is that racial tension and racially inappropriate behaviors do not necessarily flow from racism.[2] I realize this may seem like begging the question, so I ask that you bear with me for a moment.

Lawrence Blum, in his book *"I'm Not a Racist, But . . ."*, defines racist motives as those based in antipathy toward or "inferiorizing of a racial group."[3] Although I suspect most people would agree that the employees' behavior toward this executive is inappropriate, no evidence exists to suggest that they dislike him or feel superior to him. They give no indication of meeting Blum's definition of racist motives.

In this organization, both the executive and the support personnel are dealing with new complexities. Staff members unaccustomed to a racially diverse workforce at the most senior levels now must change their assumptions about and habitual responses to African-Americans. Similarly, the executive must address the complexity of being the lone African-American senior leader. Key questions for him become, How *should* I be treated as an executive? How do I *wish* to be treated? How will I *insist* on being treated? With these new complexities, diversity tension follows naturally, regardless of whether racism is present.

What, then, should this African-American pioneer do? In the context of this discussion, one thing he should *not* do is throw around accusations of racism, since he possesses no direct knowledge of the staff's motives. Little is to be gained by addressing suspicions of racism.

If he finds the behavior offensive, he should focus on stopping it. To do that, he can draw on a range of options, from accepting it (while the guard is escorting him to his office, he can begin a friendly chat about the weather or the local sports teams) to seeking relief from other senior executives. If he decides to remain with the company, he will need to be able to make quality decisions despite this real and uncomfortable—albeit natural—tension.

Is it fair for a person of color to have to endure an insulting routine that white executives do not? Of course not. But it is not surprising, given the natural caution among strangers, particularly among those who look different. Indeed, one could argue that this man's reaction falls in the same category as his challenger's behavior.

My point is this: It is highly likely that tension will accompany diversity of any kind, and people who want to address diversity effectively must keep this fact in mind. Those who dislike tension don't want to hear this discussion. They try to bypass tension or pretend it doesn't exist. Yet when they do so, the quality of the resulting decisions suffers. SDM is not about avoiding the unavoidable tensions, but rather developing the capability to make quality decisions in spite of them.

CONCEPT 4: BEING "DIVERSITY CHALLENGED" DOESN'T NECESSARILY MAKE YOU A BAD PERSON

To be diversity challenged is to have difficulty making quality decisions when differences, similarities, and tensions exist. That's it. It doesn't mean that you necessarily have a predisposition to handle diversity poorly. It says nothing necessarily about your character or mind-set. It also says nothing necessarily about motivation. It means simply that you are unable to make good decisions in the midst of diversity.

When discussing the key concepts of SDM, I usually linger on this one, for it is critical. Understanding it has an immense impact on your readiness to advance to the next diversity level. Unless you are clear about how and where you (or your organization) are diversity challenged, you won't be motivated to advance with diversity. Indeed, if you, the reader, don't see yourself as diversity challenged, you will have little motivation to finish this book.

I discovered this concept as I struggled to understand Archie Bunker of the television comedy *All in the Family.*[4] My sentiments about Archie evolved over time. At first, I agreed with those who thought the show trivialized the serious topic of racial prejudice and set back recent gains in the area of race relations. The open expressions of prejudice angered and dismayed me. The idea that someone could build a comedy on behaviors and beliefs that had harmed so many was appalling.

As the show matured, my anger evolved into a simmering resentment about the exploitation of such a serious issue. Yet I continued to watch. To my surprise, I eventually found myself viewing the show as an objective observer, accepting what was for many of us an accurate portrayal of the American scene.

Then acceptance gave way to a period in which I laughed heartily at Archie, sympathized with him, or even empathized with his views, although I in no way endorsed his thinking. At this point, I asked myself, "What's going on? Why am I developing a strange fondness for this bigot?" My appreciation for Archie has continued to grow over the years, as I have explored the nature of diversity and gained an enhanced understanding of Archie's dynamics.

At a very fundamental level, Archie was a bigot, no doubt about it. But he was a different type of bigot. He did not exhibit the malice and hatred that I had come to associate with bigotry; in fact, he seemed to be a benign bigot who intended no harm to anyone.

Perhaps his bigotry came across as less harmful because it was not confined to race but ran the gamut of the human experience. Indeed, Archie faced multiple challenges across a wide breadth of dimensions—race, gender, ethnicity, geographic origin, economic class, sexual orientation, age, and political affiliation, just to name some of the most frequently mentioned ones. Archie grappled with diversity and its inherent differences. He was, in short, severely "diversity challenged."

Although Archie was both bigoted and diversity challenged, in real life, the two conditions are not necessarily linked together. It is possible to be a bigot and not be diversity challenged, or to be free of prejudice and still be diversity challenged. This offers one explanation as to why Archie's prejudicial behavior projected little hatred or malice. His behavior was not driven by hate, but rather by the frustration of being unable to effectively address a growing number of diversity concerns. Nothing was as he had expected, and that exasperated Archie. His desire for predictability was at the core of his existence.

Norman Lear, the show's creator, once said, "Many found Archie to be a despicable character. I did not. I saw him simply as a man struggling to deal with change." In a time of rapid change, Archie's prejudicial expressions conveyed little hate because they were really cries for help from a proud and confused man, a man increasingly uncomfortable with the realities of the present.

Unquestionably, Archie became a caricature of the rest of us, since people can be inept in the presence of diversity and uncomfortable with change. As such, he can serve as a mirror and an opportunity to explore important realities about this uncomfortable condition we are all afflicted with, to one degree or another.

Six Lessons Learned from Archie Bunker

1. *"Diversity challenged" tends to be a two-way street.* If person A is diversity challenged with respect to person B, then B is likely to be diversity challenged with respect to A. The two don't know quite what to do with each other. Archie was diversity challenged with respect to Edith, his wife; Gloria, his daughter; and Michael (the "Meathead"), his son-in-law. He was particularly clueless in regard to Michael and Gloria, and the show played off their differences, similarities, and tensions.

Interestingly, Edith was more diversity challenged with Archie than he was with her. She found it hard to understand him. Yet she overcame her ineptness with diversity better than the others because she was focused on keeping the family intact.

Despite these dynamics, you rarely hear it said that Gloria, Meathead, and Edith were inept in the presence of diversity. Yet they didn't understand Archie any better than he understood them. If we ignored this fact, we would concentrate just on making Archie more capable of handling differences. This would be a serious flaw: We'd be only halfway through. Real progress requires helping *all* family members with their diversity challenges.

2. *Even those who are severely diversity challenged can be effective with diversity if they really must.* Although severely diversity challenged, Archie knew his personal priorities and made decisions compatible with them. Consider the following examples:

- *Remaining Alive.* Archie went through a bout of illness and ended up in the hospital needing a blood transfusion. To his shock, the only person with his blood type was an African-American woman doctor. Although taken aback, he nonetheless made the decision necessary to preserve his physical well-being—he accepted the transfusion.

- *Being a Good Husband.* Archie could rant and rave at Edith and strut around as king of his household. Yet when Edith said in one fashion or another, "Enough is enough," he would immediately toe the line. He valued being a good husband to Edith.
- *Being a Good Father.* Because Archie loved his "little girl," Gloria, he allowed Michael the Meathead to remain in his house.
- *Being a Good Neighbor.* Archie fought continuously with his African-American neighbor George Jefferson; yet he allowed Edith to maintain warm relationships with the Jefferson family. His decision to embrace his neighbors through his wife, daughter, and son-in-law probably came about because Edith's belief in neighborhood was also his own. Archie had a strong sense of what constituted a good neighborhood, albeit for him that meant one without people of color.

3. *The "isms" are not the only areas in which people are diversity challenged.* Many people are, for example, diversity challenged when faced with complexity. Working continuously in an overly complex environment can have negative consequences for both individuals and their organizations; it becomes increasingly harder to make quality decisions. Because diversity and complexity go hand in hand, it can be hard to tell which condition is making quality decision making difficult.

Since people can be diversity challenged for a number of reasons, we must be careful in diagnosing and interpreting racial incidents. In analyzing corporate-level racial conflicts, for example, it's important to know the principal cause of the dynamics. It may, in fact, be racism. But it is equally possible that individuals on both sides of the conflict lack the skills needed to work together productively. Or it could be that an overly complex environment is causing the difficulties. And, of course, it could be all of the above. Effective remedies require accurate diagnosis.

The notion of multiple causation has helped me to understand why I was laughing at Archie. I laughed not at his bigotry, but rather at that part of him that struggled with diversity and change—struggles that many of us share, independent of any prejudices we may have. Seeing his struggles, I could view him with empathy.

4. *It is important to uncover the root causes of bad behaviors.* Archie's offensive behavior persisted because neither he nor anyone else was equipped to adequately identify the root causes. People either accused him of being affiliated with the "isms" or assumed that he was. No one considered the possibility that other factors might have been in play.

As a result, efforts to change his behavior on a sustained basis failed because other root causes remained at work and undetected. Sustainable progress requires addressing *all* causal forces.

Offensive behavior remains offensive, regardless of whether it springs from real prejudices or from being diversity challenged, and no one should have to accept hurtful behaviors. However, if we are to make progress in resolving the situation effectively, it's important to establish the cause. In the United States, we have assumed that diversity challenges are grounded in the "isms" (e.g., racism, sexism, ageism) and that eliminating them will make everything okay. But there's a difference between being unwilling to make good decisions and being unable to. If our society is to make sustainable progress with diversity in general, we must acknowledge that wishing won't make it so. We'll need to address the skill needs of those who are diversity challenged.

5. *Preoccupation with eliminating racism can prevent quality decision making.* The racial preoccupation of the times inhibited the ability of Archie's friends and family to understand him or his behavior. This preoccupation fostered a general belief that racism and other "isms" controlled him, and essentially closed the door to identification and exploration of alternative explanations.

Often people are astonished when I suggest that it is possible for someone to be a racist and still be effective in addressing diversity. So I tell them this story.

A foreman at a large plant was doing a great job. He earned high marks for technical competence and for fair and impartial treatment of his employees. One day, however, a person of color reported that he saw the foreman off-site, and the foreman had refused to speak to him. As this report circulated, others told of similar experiences. Soon, people began openly saying the foreman was a racist. Still, no one disputed his effectiveness as a foreman. The question became whether to challenge him on his alleged behavior away from the plant.

My response is that he should be challenged only if the performance requirements for his job included specifics about off-site behavior. SDM prescribes keeping our eye on the goal. If the foreman is meeting requirements, let him be. Running an effective plant is the objective, whether or not the foreman is racist.

I should emphasize that SDM does not argue against fighting racism, but rather sees it as a separate agenda from the one currently facing this particular plant. The employees may elect to fight racism through other vehicles. However, the foreman's racism—real or hypothesized—is not hampering the plant's effectiveness. Therefore, fighting racism is not part of the workplace agenda. To make it so would risk hampering plant productivity unnecessarily.

6. *No one wants to admit being diversity challenged.* Just as Archie resisted the label of racist and sexist, individuals and organizations fight admitting they are diversity challenged—regardless of the cause. It is as if doing so is akin to their acknowledging to all the world that they are racists and sexists. Yet people who cannot come to grips with being diversity challenged have difficulty mustering sufficient motivation to address diversity.

When conducting a workshop, I often ask participants to do some homework for the next day. Their assignment is to explain the concept of being diversity challenged to someone who knows them well and then to ask, "Given this definition, how diversity challenged do you think I am, and where do you see me as being most challenged?"

The following day, few people are eager to share their findings. Most participants do so reluctantly, frequently only with prodding by their colleagues. Some simply refuse.

No one, for example, considered Archie to be evil or mean-spirited, or even to be motivated by an intent to be harmful. Being diversity challenged does not necessarily make you an evil person. Whether we recognize it or not, all of us are diversity challenged with respect to something significant in our lives. The tragedy is failing to acknowledge it and to assess precisely where we are diversity challenged, because this failing prevents us from developing the capability to make quality decisions despite our condition. Acknowledgment is the first step toward this capability.

Ironically, those least likely to see the need for assessment are minorities and women, who often believe they themselves have no issues with diversity. They endure diversity education and training so that white males can be "fixed." Organizational effectiveness with diversity requires the effectiveness of *all* individual contributors. Failure to include minorities and women in assessment and improvement efforts can be a major barrier to sustainable progress.

CONCEPT 5: BEING DIVERSITY CAPABLE IS THE GOAL

The end goal is to learn to become diversity capable, which means mastering the craft of making quality decisions in spite of differences, similarities, and related tensions. It means that we have learned to get out of our own way and make decisions that allow us to advance our own goals and those of our organization. It means that we learn to make quality decisions even though we may remain uncomfortable with certain components of the diversity mix that is present in our environment.

Two distinct components facilitate SDM mastery: diversity skills and diversity maturity. Diversity skills include the ability to recognize diversity mixtures, analyze them, and select the appropriate response. Diversity maturity—or the ability to use the diversity skills effectively—comes with wisdom, judgment, and experience.

The relationship between diversity skills and diversity maturity is not unlike that between driving skills and driving maturity. By the age of twelve, I had acquired the basic skills needed to drive a car. I could reach the pedals, see over the hood, and hold the car on the road. But I did not have driving maturity—that is, the wisdom, judgment, and experience to use the driving skills effectively—until around the age of twenty-two.

As with driving, diversity skills can be acquired more quickly and easily than diversity maturity. Skills can be taught directly through training. Acquiring maturity requires observation, introspection, and continuous learning from experiences. Diversity skills and maturity are discussed in more detail in Chapter 10.

The good news is that it does not matter where or with what dimension (e.g., race, gender, age, or sexual orientation) you become diversity capable. Once acquired, diversity capability can be used with all other dimensions. Diversity capability is universal.

IN CONCLUSION . . .

As you must recognize by now, I believe that people and organizations can become diversity capable by gaining mastery with SDM. The five concepts discussed here, and the five fundamentals presented in the next chapter, can be fashioned into a decision-making process that will allow you to become diversity capable, so you can go to the next level with diversity.

STRATEGIC DIVERSITY MANAGEMENT

FIVE FUNDAMENTALS

_____
_____

THIS CHAPTER IS THE MIDDLE PLANK of a three-part description of the craft of Strategic Diversity Management (SDM). Chapter 7 focused on the five core concepts that form the base for the craft. This chapter discusses five fundamental understandings that promote effectiveness in mastering it. Together, they undergird the craft's decision-making framework, which serves as the implementation tool. This tool, presented in detail in Chapter 9, is designed to allow organizational leaders and individual participants to approach diversity in a structured, disciplined way.

FUNDAMENTAL 1

A Shared Understanding of Core Concepts Must Be Established

Before decision making begins, there must first be a shared understanding of the core diversity concepts. Although this assertion might appear to be obvious, it isn't always.

When visiting organizations, I'm often reminded of a friend of mine—a college chaplain who, at the beginning of each school year, schedules a short meeting with each incoming freshman. Most of them, he says, have given little thought to clarifying their religious beliefs. Some push forward with whatever they learned as children. Others state, somewhat sheepishly, that they "don't believe in God."

My friend asks members of the first group whether they are open to examining their beliefs to see which still "work" and which might be revised in light of their newly adult status. He asks the second group, "Can you describe the God you don't believe in?" His purpose in both instances is to motivate students to become clear about what they believe or reject in this emotionally charged area of their lives. Such clarity, he notes, will do much to help them mature and sustain themselves in times of an inevitable crisis.

In many organizations, executives and internal diversity leaders, both individually and collectively, share the same kind of conceptual confusion—except that their confusion concerns diversity. Some go forward with their version of diversity with no inclination to examine its effectiveness. Others cannot cite the definitions and principles that undergird their efforts, so they fall back on the "diversity means different things to different people" rationale, as if it were an excuse for murky thinking.

People in both groups brush off my questions. Instead, they move quickly to talk about the "best practices" activities and interventions they have adopted. When pressed further for undergirding definitions and principles, they offer conflicting statements about the conceptual and theoretical bases of their programs.

Given these realities, I'm not surprised that organizations feel "stuck" in their diversity efforts and find themselves recycling diversity programs on a periodic basis. To be sustainable and effective, diversity efforts—like all successful personal and organizational efforts—must be grounded in well-understood and articulated concepts. These concepts then work as a map that keeps diversity efforts from straying off trail. This reality carries with it the following implications:

■   *Working Knowledge.* Effective management of diversity requires a working knowledge of five core concepts (refer to Chapter 7): diversity, Strategic Diversity Management, diversity tensions, and being diversity challenged and diversity capable.

■   *Mind-set Shift.* Because the traditional definitions of diversity are so embedded in our thinking, acquiring this working knowledge begins with a mind-set shift. Individuals can achieve this shift through careful reading of this book. Within organizations, however, greater synergy and buy-in is achieved by beginning diversity efforts with an educational session on definitions and their implications. This session is not intended to build skills. Instead, it lays the groundwork for a structured, deliberate, sustainable approach to diversity, ensuring that all players are clear about key diversity concepts and prepared to make decisions about diversity issues.

■ *Continued Practice.* Once the basic concepts have been introduced, continued reinforcement of and practice in applying them are critical. Diversity capability isn't achieved by one or two educational workshops. It requires a persistent, continuous effort to understand and operationalize the diversity concepts. Without this effort, sustained progress with individual and organizational capability just won't happen.

Ironically, executives and other action-oriented individuals hesitate to commit to this kind of preliminary effort. They wish to rush through the preparing-to-do stage and move directly to "doing." Throughout the halls of their organizations, the pledge rings, "We're committed to diversity." That may be, but a commitment to diversity management *effectiveness* requires a change in mind-set and methodology.

I believe firmly that lack of conceptual clarity is a major reason why America's organizations have not overcome the challenge of sustainability that has dogged their diversity efforts for the past twenty years. It's difficult to do something well if you're not clear what you're doing.

FUNDAMENTAL 2

Context Is Key

All decisions must be appropriate for the internal and external environments in which they are made. Diversity efforts are never conducted in a vacuum. They are shaped and affected by the external environment and the organization's mission, vision, and strategy. Consequently, the basic decision-making question becomes:

> Given our purpose, our external environmental factors, our understanding of what constitutes success, and our need to maintain and advance our competitive standing, how can we identify and respond to the *critical* diversity issues that require our attention?

Notice that the question assumes that organizational leaders begin their diversity efforts *after* they're familiar with their external and internal environments and know their company's mission, vision, and strategy—all of which constitute a context. It is impossible to identify or respond adequately to critical diversity mixtures until this contextual knowledge is in place. Once they are, the issue becomes, "Which diversity mixtures have the potential to give us a strategic advantage or to hinder our ability to meet our goals?" These are the mixtures that must be addressed. The other diversity issues can safely be ignored.

Making the Compelling Business Case

How do leaders determine which diversity issues are critical? They identify and address the diversity issues for which they can make a compelling business case. Many diversity thrusts fail for lack of a solid business case.

Once, after completing a presentation, I was taken aside and asked, "What do you do when the organization commits to decisions about diversity, but a key senior executive refuses to conform?"

My response: "It may be that your organization is not as committed as it might seem at first glance. If it were, other senior leaders would shoot down the nonconforming officers." I could have said, "You don't have a compelling business rationale for your diversity decisions; otherwise, senior officers would not tolerate the nonconforming executive." Where true business issues and requirements are concerned, executives routinely punish nonconformists.

This organization's situation is not unique. Despite all the rhetoric about business rationales for diversity thrusts, rarely do I see a *compelling* business case. I do see legitimate, innovative, believable, and well-reasoned business cases, but few can compel and hold their own against other priorities.

My lightbulb moment on this subject came during a workshop. A participant asked, "What do you do when diversity is not rated a priority?"

"You make the business case," I replied.

"I did! But it doesn't stand up well against other priorities."

This exchange awakened me to how extremely difficult it is to develop a compelling business rationale for diversity efforts around workforce issues. These rationales typically fail to convince because of the relatively low strategic importance assigned to people issues. It's not that people are mistreated or abused. It's simply that many senior executives do not act as if people are strategic—even when they make statements to the contrary. If they did, the ongoing efforts of human resources departments to raise their corporate status would not be needed. Under these circumstances, building a business case for managing workforce diversity is a challenging task.

Another barrier to making a compelling case for managing workforce diversity is the prevalent politicized definition of diversity as affirmative action, and affirmative action as diversity. As long as these definitions hold sway and affirmative action remains controversial, it will remain difficult to make a compelling case for moving forward with diversity and diversity management.

This challenge is not confined to business settings. Nonprofit organizations face the same struggles. Even after recognizing that their volunteers and the people they serve are becoming more diverse, nonprofit leaders have trouble building a compelling rationale for developing a diversity management capability; as a result, their entities get caught in the I-285 cycle.

Nor are churches exempt from this problem. Even those that cite a rationale in tune with Dr. King's "ethical demands" can have difficulty with diversity and diversity management. Not long ago a friend asked me, "Roosevelt, how does this notion of diversity play itself out in churches?" I explained that churches could have diversity along any number of dimensions—race, gender, ethnicity, musical preferences, style of worship preferences, and theological beliefs.

My friend went on to say that his church was experiencing tension around race, and that he had tried to tell his fellow members that "this was just diversity." His point was, "Just as we have diversity in work settings, we can have it in our churches. We just have to learn to deal with it." Apparently they couldn't. About three months after our conversation, his pastor resigned in frustration.

Similarly, community leaders struggle to be compelling with diversity and diversity management. They say things like, "Diversity is our greatest strength," and "Diversity is the right thing to do," but these arguments do not compel or sustain progress—even when community members agree with the claims.

Using Universal Definitions

I believe there is a solution to this conundrum, and that it begins with the use of a universal definition of diversity. That's why the willingness to define diversity as any "mixture of differences, similarities, and tensions" that can exist among the elements of a pluralistic mixture is so important.

A universal definition of diversity creates the flexibility that allows leaders ultimately to acquire a diversity management capability. It makes it possible to ask, "Of all of the diversity mixtures that are critical for our mission, vision, and strategy, which one offers the strongest possibility for developing a compelling business case?"

That mixture then becomes the door through which the entity evolves its diversity management capability. Once the universal capability has been established, it can be used with any mixture—including those for which a diversity effort is needed and a compelling business case cannot be made.

> *Example.* One organization I worked with not long ago demonstrated this approach. The organization's diversity council struggled mightily to come up with a compelling business rationale for moving forward with workforce diversity. After many efforts and rejections from their workplace community, someone asked, "Are there any other diversity issues where we might make a compelling business rationale?"

One executive said, "We need more synergy between two of our product lines. That is a diversity issue." Another executive noted that two years before, the organization had decided to grow globally, and that many diversity issues had already emerged. Another executive said, "We also decided strategically to grow through acquisitions and mergers. From past experience, we know that can mean plenty of diversity."

The executives decided to construct their business rationale for developing a diversity management capability around one of these issues, with the idea of subsequently revisiting workforce concerns. They saw this decision not as a retreat from workforce diversity, but rather as exploiting the area where they had the greatest opportunity to make the necessary compelling business case.

Not everyone would agree—with the definition or the council's decision. Some people are uneasy with the idea of using a universal definition and the prospect of addressing multiple diversity mixtures. They're concerned about two possibilities: that the mixture they see as most important won't get addressed, and that addressing more than one mixture at a time might entail more complexity than they can handle.

The folks concerned about the first possibility are the most vocal. They often retreat to a tenacious, single-minded focus on their diversity issue of choice. Cora Daniels, author of *Black Power Inc.,* gives voice to this position. "Diversity in today's watered-down, one-size-fits-all form is flawed," she writes. To buttress her point, Daniels quotes the views of a diversity champion, or advocate: "Diversity has to leave out race for it to be valued in corporate America. Any diversity person will say we don't just look at race—we look at a number of factors. This tells you they've discounted race."[1]

Yet neither concern is warranted. Nothing in the universal definition of diversity prevents an organization from addressing its favorite issue, and the injunction that only *critical* diversity issues should be addressed greatly reduces rather than increases the universe of mixtures to be addressed.

Keeping Diversity Neutral

Inherently, diversity is neither good nor bad. It all depends on context. Many people are shocked when I say this. People subscribing to the "diversity is inherently good" philosophy can be offended.

Yet it is important to look at the facts. Truth be told, under certain conditions, some types of diversity offer no benefits at all. In fact, they may offer negatives. In these situations, effective management of diversity means minimizing or eliminating these negatives. Again, the appropriateness of exclusion or inclusion as a response depends not on personal philosophy but on context.

It's easier to understand if we look at what organizations do rather than what they say. Corporate downsizings, for example, frequently serve as a vehicle for excluding talents and skills that are no longer needed because of changes in a company's mission, vision, or strategy. In fact, organizations routinely acquire previously unsought professional capabilities while laying off individuals whose capabilities no longer mesh with their mission, vision, or strategy.

Within the universal definition of diversity, the statement that "Diversity is neutral" is easy to accept. It is only within the context of the politicized definition of diversity, where it solely conveys the presence of multiple races in the workforce, that the statement becomes untenable, in light of our country's history with discrimination and slavery.

FUNDAMENTAL 3

Diversity Efforts Must Be Requirements Driven

Since quality decisions must often be made amid diversity tension, and since all of us are diversity challenged to at least some degree, it is critical to be able to focus on essentials. It allows us to home in on what is important and to make quality decisions in spite of tensions and challenges.

That's why diversity efforts must be requirements driven. That is, they must focus on what is absolutely necessary to accomplish the individual's or the organization's mission, vision, and strategy. Requirements differ from traditions (the way things have always been done), personal preferences (the way I like things to be), and conveniences (the way that is easiest for me). Instead, requirements are "the way things absolutely must be."

Neither executives nor individual contributors are always clear about requirements. On many occasions, I have been asked, "How do you determine what the requirements really are?" The following exchange is typical:

> *Example.* At the end of a workshop, a CEO addressed his direct reports. "I don't believe we know what our requirements are," he said. "The world is changing; our industry is changing; and our company is changing. Surely, our requirements must be changing as well. But what are they?"
>
> He offered an example: "If you want to advance into senior management, you have to have a spouse." With fourteen men and one woman around the table, someone more accurately stated, "You have to have a wife, and she has to fit a profile." All heads nodded. The CEO asked, "Is that a requirement?" The room remained quiet.
>
> Someone else noted: "If you wish to be in senior management, senior managers must know you in the context of your golf game, as well as the context of work. So, when we have recreational days, people.compete to play golf with a senior manager."
>
> Another executive asked, "What about young people? Some of them appear determined to never play golf." One of his colleagues responded, "That's their tough luck." Another person countered, "That's our tough luck! You mean we cannot access talent just because a person won't get on the golf course?"
>
> The CEO asked, "Is that a requirement?" Again the room remained quiet. "I think," the CEO proposed, "that we ought to come back for a day or two to sort out our requirements. I don't think we know what they are."

Entities other than corporations struggle with being requirements driven. Not long ago, representatives of an East Coast university asked me to consult with them on designing a change process. Many ideas about change were discussed, and many agreements made. At the end of the day, I was invited to attend a convocation service at the chapel. The service featured the university's hymn, whose lyrics contained numerous mentions of the institution's "rich traditions." I immediately recognized that, for this university, change would be an uphill struggle.

Communities also grapple with differentiating requirements from traditions and preferences as they wrestle with culture wars. At base, debates about same-sex marriages, affirmative action, abortion, curriculum issues, and immigration are a community's way of determining its core requirements.

Families are not immune. After one presentation, I asked a woman in attendance if the material discussed would be helpful with her work responsibilities. "I have no idea," she replied, "but I just can't wait to get home and talk with my daughter! A lot of our conflict has been over preferences and not requirements. I'm clear about that now."

Becoming requirements driven is not easy. It's not like flipping a switch. In our society, we have become accustomed to having our personal preferences met. Consider these few examples:

Example 1. A friend of mine was unhappy when I spoke of requirements. "You aren't saying I cannot gravitate toward my friends, are you?" I responded, "If you are running a friendship society, the SDM craft says you gravitate toward friends; otherwise, you focus on requirements."

Example 2. A senior executive said that he understood my comments about requirements, preferences, traditions, and conveniences. However, he felt that he was more effective if his direct reports were not only competent but also his friends. He had made his personal preference of friendship a requirement, and he was uncertain he wanted to abandon that practice.

Example 3. I talked about "foxhole diversity" with a group of executives. A soldier has dug a foxhole and is trying to decide who should join him in the hole. As he hears enemy fire around him, he asks a few questions: Does each candidate have all of his faculties? Does each have a gun? Does each know how to shoot? Does each have the will to shoot?

The questions have nothing to do with race, gender, geographic origin, sexual orientation, or religion. Just, can the person do the job?

One of the most senior executives raised his hand and said, "Be clear! In my foxhole, I want someone who has his or her faculties, possesses a gun, can shoot, will shoot, *and* meets my preferences."

I countered, "Whose preferences count?" He replied, "I know what I am saying. Candidly, I am not ready for a requirements-driven organization."

Three-Step Process

For those of us who *are* ready for such an enterprise (whether at the corporate, community, nonprofit, or family level), becoming requirements driven is a three-step process.

1. Identify your requirements in the context of the mission, vision, and strategy of yourself and/or your enterprise.

2. Agree to be driven by requirements; then refuse to fall back on preferences, traditions, and conveniences.

3. Accept differences in the area of nonrequirements.

At issue is this: Is the decision maker, whether leader or enterprise member, willing to put the achievement of an important goal before personal whim or self-interest? Without this willingness, the tyranny of personal preferences, traditions, and conveniences will continue.

FUNDAMENTAL 4

Diversity Aspirations of Individuals and Their Enterprises Must Be Considered

Typically, when we speak of diversity, we speak from the perspective of the enterprise or the manager as its representative. Rarely do we think of the personal aspirations of individual leaders or contributors. Yet, clearly, the aspirations of these individuals may differ considerably from that of their enterprise. Equally clearly, the aspirations of individuals can impact the effectiveness of an enterprise's diversity efforts.

As members of any enterprise (e.g., a corporation, community group, or family, as the case might be), *individuals* must be clear about both their own *and* their organization's diversity aspirations. This is true whether they are acting as agents of the enterprise or as independent contributors. Understanding both perspectives and where they mesh and differ allows people to think clearly and to make quality decisions for themselves and their enterprises.

Decision makers must be clear about their enterprise's diversity aspirations and the extent to which they are shared by leaders and individual contributors. In doing so, they must, of course, first specify the enterprise's mission, vision, strategy, and related requirements. Once this is done, they should ask themselves two sets of questions—on *representational* diversity and *behavioral* diversity—to clarify how much and what kind of diversity they want. Once they know, they should introduce the questions to everyone in the enterprise for reflection and response. Only then will they know if they are ready to begin formal diversity efforts or if more groundwork must be done.

Why two kinds of questions? Representational questions refer to who or what should be in the mixture. Behavioral questions refer to the amount of behavioral differences that are sought within the mixture. It is quite possible to desire representational diversity without seeking behavioral diversity.

The following questions will, if thoughtfully answered, allow organizations and individuals to "get honest" about their aspirations.

Representational Diversity

Of the two types of diversity questions, by far the most common is representational. Consider the following illustration:

Do we want representational diversity?
Yes.

If so, what kind?
The managers decide to seek representation with respect to race, gender, and military veteran status.

If so, how much?
This is where many corporations struggle. To specify a numerical target risks being perceived as establishing quotas, which are politically and legally unacceptable. So, often leaders do not identify how much. A consequence is that no one knows what success means.

How do we achieve the desired representation?
The leaders agree to make certain that the organization recruits where the available applicant pools contain sufficient racial, gender, and veteran representation.

To what extent have we already achieved the desired representation?
Here, the leaders count and compare the results to their aspirations, assuming they can agree on what would constitute success.

Behavioral Diversity

Much less common are the behavioral diversity questions. Here is a hypothetical example of how they would go. I speak hypothetically because I have never seen these questions raised formally.

Do we want behavioral variations?
Yes.

If so, what kind?
Managers express a desire for behavioral variation with respect to thinking styles and personality. Stated differently, they want some mavericks.

If so, how much?

Again, managers have the same challenge as with representational questions. While there are no legal restrictions—to my knowledge—regarding diversity quotas with respect to thinking style and personality, I suspect that concerns around race and gender quotas might generate an overall aversion to numerical targets. Yet, the more specific managers can be about their aspirations, the greater their opportunity for success.

How do we go about achieving the desired level of behavioral variations?

Managers can use formal and informal means for identifying qualified applications. References represent one example of the informal, while legal and otherwise appropriate instruments could be used formally to identify qualified individuals in regard to thinking style and personality. With respect to thinking styles, some educational and training interventions might be used with current associates to attain a higher level of behavioral variation.

Even where managers and associates are clear they want diversity along these maverick lines, unless they are diversity capable, their ability to accept this behavioral variation is likely to be relatively limited.

To what extent have we already achieved the desired level of behavioral variations?

Managers committed to greater thinking style and personality diversity would develop a way to assess the existing associates along these lines, and if they can agree as to what is desirable, then compare their "actual" and "desired" levels.

Decision makers often don't ask about individual aspirations when planning a diversity effort, nor do they ask the behavioral diversity questions. They tend to focus only on representation concerns, which limits both the people and the questions they ask. Ultimately, it stifles the success of their diversity efforts.

The failure to ask the behavioral diversity questions is universal. I have yet to see an enterprise formally consider them. It is not because they don't want this diversity. People say with conviction that they desire and need "diversity of thought" or "diversity of thinking styles." Yet they never use the behavioral aspiration questions in developing selection criteria. They assume instead that if they have representational diversity along dimensions such as race, gender, age, and sexual orientation, the desired behavioral variety will follow.

This is not necessarily true. Racial and gender representation means that multiple races and both genders participate in the mixture. But it does not necessarily say anything about the behavioral variety they will generate.

Enterprises shortchange themselves with these practices. Quality decision making requires being clear about individual and enterprise aspirations in traditional and nontraditional representation areas, and with respect to behavioral diversity aspirations.

FUNDAMENTAL 5

Enterprises and Individuals Must Apply SDM Universally

To manage diversity effectively, enterprises and individuals must apply the craft of Strategic Diversity Management to whatever mixture is critical. Of course, this is easier said than done. Awareness, acceptance, and understanding of SDM do not translate necessarily into implementation. It is possible to understand and accept SDM's definitions and principles and yet be unable to use them outside of the classroom.

One senior executive attended briefings on SDM three separate times. When his colleagues joked with him about being too "dense" to pick up SDM, he responded, "This is important material, but I keep losing it once I leave the workshop. I am trying to retain the substance."

One reason for the difficulty is that SDM thinking is not widely used, especially in comparison to the traditional affirmative action approach. As a result, once the executive left the briefing, he was immersed in an environment where implementing SDM meant going against the grain.

His case is not unusual. Effective implementation of SDM requires an ability to manage change. That's because it will be necessary to change the organization's grain so that its internal environment becomes receptive to SDM's definitions and principles. Companies will need to examine and modify their culture, as well as certain systems and policies. To neglect this change process dooms any implementation effort with SDM to a short life.

Without such facilitative change, leaders will work hard on implementation, only to tire from fighting the established mind-set. Often, they will be unaware of the environmental barriers and will conclude that SDM is just too difficult and unrealistic. In this circumstance, the problem is not SDM, but rather the essence of the enterprise.

In a different but equally damaging scenario, after trying conscientiously to implement SDM "against the grain," weary diversity champions declare victory and look for the next "fad" or "best practices" silver bullet. In the meantime, the whole notion of diversity loses credibility. In sum, going against the grain is not an option. Changing the grain is a must.

No matter how compatible with SDM an organization's environment is, effectiveness with the framework process (described in the next chapter) will require practice. One of the most productive ways to gain readiness and capability with universal applications is to practice, practice, practice.

Yet few enterprises take the time to set up practice sessions. Not uncommonly, senior leaders roll out formal education and training sessions without any provision for meaningful sustained practice applications. It is as if they hope that learning will take hold by osmosis or some magical force. This simply will not happen. Formal, deliberate practice is essential, especially when implementation goes against the organization's grain.

This practice can be directed toward a wide variety of real diversity challenges that have been addressed previously or with diversity concerns that are still in play. There should be many practice sessions, and it should be clear that their purpose is to prepare managers and associates for full adoption and utilization of SDM. The goal is to leave the practice field ready to play the game.

IN CONCLUSION . . .

If developing a universal diversity capability sounds as if it requires forethought and effort, that's because it does. Yet I am convinced that the results are worth it.

It is essential that America's enterprises (defined broadly) develop a universal diversity capability. Such a capability would, at the very least, help enterprises avoid the round-robin syndrome, where leaders scamper to address diversity dimensions in a sequential, silo fashion. Typically, in this pattern, one year is devoted to one particular dimension, with subsequent years being devoted to the remaining issues one at a time. Frequently, by the time the enterprise has touched all the dimensional bases, its leaders must begin the cycle again—because conditions have degenerated as the spotlight moved.

A capability to address multiple mixtures with one overarching universal approach would make it possible to realize simultaneous progress on multiple fronts. Only when this happens will America's organizations become "unstuck" with their diversity efforts.

STRATEGIC DIVERSITY MANAGEMENT

THE DECISION-MAKING PROCESS AT TJAX COMPANY

IF A PICTURE IS WORTH A THOUSAND WORDS, then a concrete example is worth a thousand words about theory. At the heart of this chapter is a story, a workplace example involving diversity of corporate functions. Although it is fictionalized, the story represents a composite of several real-life situations I have encountered in my work as a consultant. As you observe the participants in the story struggling to make good decisions, you will watch them using a key diversity management tool: a decision-making process.

The process is based on the key concepts and fundamentals described in the preceding two chapters. It is a straightforward, step-by-step process—broad enough to be useful in a wide range of circumstances, and specific enough to bring diversity management to a very real, very tangible level. What is particularly rewarding for me is that as people work through these steps to arrive at good decisions, they are also, without quite being aware of it, enhancing their level of diversity skill and maturity, two essentials (discussed in the next chapter) that come only with practice. It's almost magic. This is a great example of the potential of practice to lead to greater capability.

Some readers, oriented toward action, may be tempted to skip this chapter and move forward on their own. That's a possibility, of course, but I don't recommend it. It would be a bit like teaching yourself to play golf. There's a reason why self-taught golfers quickly become big advocates of formal instruction for beginners. With diversity management, the stakes are considerably higher.

THE SCENARIO

Three friends from graduate school joined the Tjax Company on exactly the same day. Although they had decided independently to work there, each looked forward to being associated with each other professionally as well as socially.

The three had collaborated before. They possessed significantly different undergraduate backgrounds—art, engineering, and political science—but they had hit it off well from the beginning of their MBA program. Over the two years of study, they had worked on three or four projects together, blending their separate specialties of research, marketing, and production.

Their families had become friends as well. Each man had entered the MBA program married and with young children. Over time, their families became a close-knit social and academic support system. Wives and children were all happy about joining the local company.

Roughly ten years old when the trio joined, Tjax was known as a rapidly growing company and a great place for young business talent to grow in expertise and prosperity. It was this reputation that attracted the three friends. When they were hired, Tjax was preparing for unprecedented growth and was seeking more formally trained, professional management in the very areas of their disciplines. Their projections proved accurate. Tjax grew phenomenally in the five years following the friends' employment.

Soon, the organization went public, and the three people who had originally headed up research, production, and marketing left the company as wealthy individuals. Over the next twelve months, the friends were promoted to take their places. Since Tjax's projections for the next ten years were as upbeat as the first fifteen years had been, the friends looked forward to "great things."

As the three friends assumed their new roles as heads of their respective functional units, Tjax had just completed a new generation of technological advances that offered great sales potential. No one doubted the company's revenue would grow.

A strategic plan was developed. Marketing's job in the early stages would be to sell the new technology to customers and to explore opportunities for application. Once an opportunity was identified, marketing would work with research to develop the necessary specifications. Research in turn would forward the completed specifications to production, which would then manufacture the products.

Company executives anticipated considerable customized work for the first two or three years. Marketing, research, and production would need to be tightly integrated—more than ever before in the company's history. Since the three new function heads had a tight bond of friendship and experience working together, they assumed that achieving the required integration would be a snap.

The three friends were positioned to play a major role in Tjax's future development. Delighted that each of them had reached the head of their units simultaneously, the three anticipated the joy of working together. Unfortunately, the reality turned out to be quite different.

To their surprise, their relationships deteriorated shortly after their promotions. At work, they frequently clashed and disagreed contentiously. Their interactions generated so much stress that all three developed physical ailments. One lost his hair, another developed stomach ulcers, and the third suffered from sleep disorders. They were truly puzzled as to why their friendships were in such bad repair.

Other senior executives were just as bewildered. They had anticipated that the demands for greater integration would produce some stressful situations, but they had expected that the bonds of friendship would help the new managers through the challenge. Some company leaders wondered aloud if they had made a mistake, and if so, how they might make things right. The three friends were in real danger of being fired.

The wives were startled and indeed horrified by developments among their husbands. They got together to talk things over and decided to insist that the husbands seek some third-party intervention, whether through Tjax or privately. "Fifteen years of friendship warrants at least that minimum investment," they said. The three men agreed and thus began their adventure with the decision-making framework.

STEP 1: SPECIFY CONTEXT

To explore the context within which decisions must be made means, at a minimum, to identify mission, vision, strategy, and requirements. In many cases, it means exploring the external environment as well. This step relates back to fundamental 2 (context is key) and fundamental 3 (diversity efforts must be requirements driven), as presented in Chapter 8.

With respect to Tjax, the overall *mission* is to grow the company by maintaining existing product lines and exploiting the new technology's potential. The three friends might have described their mission as "making the quality decisions necessary to support the company's fifteen-year-old product lines, and generating the functional integration required to exploit its new technology."

The company's overall *vision* might be stated as "continued revenue and profit growth through existing product lines and the new technology." For the three friends, the vision likely would be "effective functional integration in support of old and new product lines."

Tjax's *strategy* is to develop and exploit the new technology as its expected source of competitive advantage. The three friends' strategic contribution would be to achieve the level of integration necessary to exploit the new technology.

The principal *requirement,* based on Tjax's mission, vision, and strategy, would be the exploitation of the new technology. At a general, overarching level, this requirement is a must if the company is to realize its mission, vision, and strategy. For the friends, the requirement—their absolute must—is to achieve the necessary level of integration.

STEP 2: IDENTIFY MIXTURE COMPONENTS

The task here is to analyze the critical diversity mixture and to learn as much as possible about its components. This task follows from fundamental 1 (a shared understanding of core diversity concepts; described in Chapter 8). Key questions are:

- Who (what) is in the mixture?

- What are the differences and similarities among the components of the mixture?

- What are the agendas and priorities of the components?

- What are the "requirements" of each component?

Let's see what happens when we apply these questions to the Tjax scenario.

Who is in the mixture? In this case, there are three people and their families. Each of the three is head of a major Tjax function: production, marketing, and research. Individually, the friends are married with children.

What are their differences and similarities? A number of differences exist among the three principal players, including:
- Different undergraduate degrees
- Different MBA concentrations
- Different functional areas of expertise and experience

As a result of these differences, we can assume that, in some areas of life, the three friends probably have distinctively different views of the world. But the friends share many similarities as well. Key similarities are:
- Graduate degrees from the same school
- Exact same tenure with Tjax
- Desire for success and upward mobility
- Prior success with the company
- Their friendship (a company and personal asset)
- Families (wives and children)
- Willingness to mix work and social relationships

What are their priorities? They have four critical priorities: (1) Continue their personal growth with Tjax, (2) achieve the necessary functional integration, (3) maintain the integrity of their functional operations, and (4) preserve their friendships.

We do not know for sure how the three friends would rank

these priorities, but we can guess. They have been focused and task oriented from their time together in graduate school. While they want to continue their friendship, they likely place a priority on their professional obligations. Their wives, of course, may assign different priorities.

What are their requirements? In this instance, the friends' priorities are their requirements. The men want to achieve their professional objectives and also maintain their friendships. They do not want one without the other, and their families reinforce these aspirations. They want it all.

STEP 3: ASSESS DIVERSITY TENSIONS

The task in this step is to understand the tensions that have been generated by the mixture. It requires looking at the following variables: nature, source (i.e., cause), diversity-challenged condition, intensity, and costs. This step also flows from fundamental 1 (a shared understanding of core concepts must be established).

Nature. The tension here has to do with decision making as the three colleagues try to achieve functional integration. It has been manifested in clashes of opinion and contentious disagreement, and it has also been expressed in physical ailments: hair loss, stomach ulcers, and sleep disorders.

Source (Cause). Several factors have contributed to this tension. One is the complexity of achieving integration. The three friends must make integration decisions involving (1) the perspectives of three significantly different functional areas, (2) the customers' expectations and requirements, and (3) the embryonic characteristics of a new technology.

A second cause is that the three principals were unprepared for the tension. Previously, the need for integration was much lower, so the three friends had relatively little experience with intense integrative decisions. In addition, their long friendships probably left them vulnerable and unprepared for intense tension. Because they were friends, they were more likely to take the tensions personally and experience an even higher level of stress.

A third cause of tension is that company executives apparently had no framework for thinking about their situation. They were unprepared experientially or intellectually for the tensions associated with managing a functional mixture characterized by differences, similarities, and tensions. Regardless of who headed the functions, tensions would exist because of the complexity and the different perspectives involved. However, neither the executives nor the three friends understood this fact. As a result, the friends received little assistance from company leaders.

Diversity-Challenged Condition. The combination of circumstances left the friends severely diversity challenged with respect to making quality decisions. Indeed, they give little evidence of being qualified to head the units under the present circumstances, even though they would have been eminently qualified before the new technology and its requirement for greater integration. Under present conditions, unless they can get around being diversity challenged, they should be receptive to reassignments, for they are placing Tjax's strategy to gain competitive edge at risk.

Intensity. The intensity level is high, precisely because of the strategic importance of the three friends' roles. Their performance will be key to Tjax's strategic failure or success. The threats to their personal sense of competency, friendships, and their families' support network heighten the intensity.

Costs. The prevailing tension threatens to be very costly. It could prevent achieving the necessary integration, damage further the physical health of the three friends, harm their friendships, and severely strain their families' professional and social support network.

STEP 4: IDENTIFY DESIRED STATE

This step recognizes the truism that you have to identify what you want before you can figure out how to achieve it. Here, the company and the principal players must make sure they understand what the desired state would look like: its nature (i.e., what constitutes a successful outcome), the benefits it would offer, and the factors that would hinder or help its achievement.

Step 4 grows out of diversity fundamentals 3 and 4, which call for being requirements driven and identifying individual and organizational aspirations (see Chapter 8). These requirements and aspirations represent significant elements of the desired end state, and any decisions that are made must satisfy them.

Nature. For Tjax, the desired state (i.e., what it wants to achieve) has several key elements:
- The three critical functions are able to perform their respective tasks well.
- The three critical functions achieve the integration around customers' needs that are required for exploiting the new technology.
- Customers are delighted with both the processes and products made possible by the new technology.
- The company enjoys phenomenal growth that is comparable to the success Tjax experienced during its first ten years.
- Stockholders are happy and thriving.

For the three friends, the desired state also has several aspects, some of which overlap with those of the corporation:
- Individually, each function effectively supports the existing product lines and the new technology.
- Collectively, the three functions achieve the functional integration required to exploit the new technology.
- The three friends achieve the required integration with minimal physical ailments.
- The three friends cope effectively with the physical stress that may persist.
- Tjax customers are satisfied.
- Tjax enjoys prosperity comparable to that of its first ten years.
- Individually, the three friends enjoy growing personal prosperity.

■   The three friends preserve their friendships and their families' support network.

Benefits Offered. From the company's perspective, the desired state ensures continuation of Tjax's reign as a "corporation on the move" in terms of revenue and profits, and maintains the confidence of investors who bought the recently offered stock. Further strategic success would position Tjax to develop the next wave of technology that could serve as the basis for the company's next growth stage.

Professionally, for the three friends, the desired state promises an opportunity to grow in managerial capability, to position themselves for a CEO office, and to realize financial security at a relatively young age. The prosperity associated with the desired state would give them significant professional and lifestyle flexibility. Unquestionably, the desired state has much to offer these three colleagues.

Hindering Factors. The fact that the three friends are both individually and collectively diversity challenged with respect to functional diversity poses the greatest threat to achieving the desired state. Particularly damaging is the friends' lack of a framework with which to address their diversity-challenged condition. Indeed, no one seems to realize he is diversity challenged. They must collectively and individually enhance their capabilities with respect to functional integration.

Furthermore, they cannot limit the task to themselves. No evidence exists that their associates are any better prepared for the integration task than are their leaders. The three must empower their functions to become diversity capable, too. Only when the three leaders and their associates become diversity capable with respect to functional integration will they achieve this goal.

Facilitating Factors. The most encouraging facilitating factor is the wives' encouragement for the friends to slow the process down and to seek third-party intervention. Without this slowing down, the friends likely would continue to rely on their common sense and limited experience with integration, thus increasing the probability of a continued freefall into personal and professional disaster.

If the friends can secure help, the reassurance that their situation is not new and that there are frameworks for coping (including the Strategic Diversity Management Process) will be facilitating factors. Should they be presented with the Strategic Diversity Management (SDM) craft, their biggest challenge will be to recognize they are dealing with a diversity issue.

STEP 5: SELECT RESPONSES

The ultimate goal of SDM is to help people make a quality decision even when they are faced with differences, similarities, and related tensions. That decision should be congruent with the realities discussed in steps 1 through 4.

Which options have been used previously? To this point, the friends have not proactively chosen a response because they haven't recognized that they are struggling with a diversity issue. Apparently, they have relied on common sense and experience.

In retrospect, it's easy to see that their response has been grossly inadequate. Yet the three—all confident and successful managers—must have believed it was legitimate. Nothing warned them that they were entering a zone for which they were not prepared. They accepted their new positions amid celebrations of their successes and capabilities. The challenge of achieving integration (i.e., diversity management) blindsided them individually and collectively.

What benefits have been realized from the previous approach? Essentially, none. They have made little, if any, progress with the necessary integration tasks. Indeed, their bosses are now considering removing the three friends from their positions and replacing them.

Given the benefits realized so far, what issues remain to be addressed? Since nothing has been resolved regarding integration, all related issues remain to be addressed. The friends need help.

Which options offer the greatest likelihood for gain? Without exposure to SDM, the friends have four basic options:

1. *Continue the status quo.* In this case, the status quo cannot be continued. To do so would prevent progress and result in the friends' losing their jobs.

2. *Adopt a "your turn, my turn" compromise approach to decision making.* Undertaken for the sake of friendship, this approach would bring about a more congenial atmosphere, and from time to time, it may produce optimal decisional making. It could also produce a disaster should a decision of the "rotational winner" be flawed. This form of compromise decision making is less invested in meeting the "requirements" of the situation than in ensuring that everyone gets a turn at decision making.

3. *Adopt a "go along to get along" approach to decision making.* This approach represents another compromise option, again, for sake of friendship. Its principal focus is not the dictates of "requirements," but rather what is necessary to get along. Obviously, this practice could also result in flawed decisions.

4. *Seek a third-party intervention.* The third-party intervention holds the greatest promise of gain, especially if the consultant is grounded in SDM. An SDM intervention would:

    ■ Help the friends recognize that functional integration is a diversity issue.

    ■ Introduce a decision-making framework based on requirements.

    ■ Help the friends acquire the diversity management skills and diversity maturity needed to use the framework effectively. (Chapter 10 discusses diversity management skills and diversity maturity in the context of Tjax's three friends.)

Even a third party who is unfamiliar with SDM, but has experience in bringing other frameworks to bear on complex issues, could help them to make some progress. At a minimum, a third-party intervention would interrupt the dysfunctional practice of expecting different results while continuing the same practices.

IN CONCLUSION . . .

I believe that the best possibility of success for our friends is the Strategic Diversity Management craft. This craft fashions the diversity concepts and fundamentals into a structured framework that enhances the ability to solve problems and make decisions around diversity issues.

There is another important benefit: In addition to providing structure, the framework can "buy time." Its use can slow the dynamics of a diversity issue, giving time for reflection and thus minimizing the likelihood that matters will spiral out of control.

STRATEGIC DIVERSITY MANAGEMENT

FOUNDATION FOR SUCCESS

IMAGINE THAT YOU ASK to borrow my car so that you can visit an out-of-state friend. I smile and hand you the keys, a gasoline credit card, and my auto club card.

You're happily surprised. "Thanks! I'll see you later."

"Not so fast," I say. "First, you need to show me that you have the driving skills and maturity to bring my car home undamaged."

"What do you mean?"

"By driving skills, I mean that you know how to start the car and navigate it legally down the road. By driving maturity, I mean that you have the experience, judgment, and wisdom to complement your skills—to make good decisions, to handle things that might come up, to deal appropriately with all kinds of driving situations. I need to see your license as proof of skills and the names of references who can attest to your driving maturity. Then you can have the car."

To this point, the discussion of Strategic Diversity Management as a learnable craft has been the equivalent of providing you with an automobile. The key concepts and fundamental understandings presented in Chapters 7 and 8 are, in effect, the car. The decision-making framework described in Chapter 9 (within the context of the Tjax case study) is the equivalent of a map for your trip, guiding you on every leg of your journey. But if you wish to use SDM optimally, you need more than just the car and the map. You also need skills of diversity management and diversity maturity. They are essential; without them, you cannot use SDM effectively.

Once again, using our friends from Tjax Company as an example, I briefly describe these two critical traits.

DIVERSITY MANAGEMENT SKILLS

Three skills are critical in mastering the craft of SDM:

1. Being able to recognize a diversity mixture

2. Knowing how to determine whether action is needed

3. Knowing how to select and use the appropriate action option

Being Able to Recognize a Diversity Mixture

If you can't see a situation as a diversity mixture, you can't address it as such. The three Tjax executives, for example, first have to acknowledge individually and collectively that they constitute a diversity mixture. From an outsider's perspective, this might seem to be a no-brainer, but in reality, several factors could make it difficult:

■ *Alternative Frameworks.* The executives have other frameworks for addressing their situation: leadership, team building, organization design, organization development, and conflict management—or any combination of those techniques. In fact, in most situations, SDM is not the only reasonable choice. Because it is the least known technique, it conceivably could be the choice of desperation—until it has a known track record of effectiveness.

■ *Lack of Awareness.* The Tjax friends may not have heard of SDM; therefore, it would not be among their options.

■ *Politicized Definition of Diversity.* If they think of diversity as a synonym for affirmative action, the friends could reject a "diversity" framework for their situation, since no apparent racial, gender, or ethnic issues are calling for attention.

■   *Emotionalism.* The more emotional the situation becomes, the less likely that the friends would recognize it as a diversity mixture or as compatible with *any* framework. They would probably get caught up in the emotionalism of the moment and never call "time out" for some type of assessment. Fortunately, their wives are calling for an intervention.

■   *Tension.* As with emotionalism, the greater the tension of the moment, the greater the danger the friends will be caught up in the dynamics of their situation and try to muddle through.

■   *Executive Pride.* Senior executives can sometimes see themselves as being all knowing—or believe they should be. If the Tjax friends hold this view, they may be unwilling to agree to a time-out.

Alone or together, all these factors can make recognizing a diversity mixture more difficult. The Tjax executives could go through their situation without ever acknowledging it as a diversity mixture.

Determining Whether Action Is Needed

Not all diversity mixtures must be addressed. Before deciding to do anything, you must determine the importance of the issue. Is the gain that can be achieved or the loss that can be prevented significant enough to merit action?

In the Tjax situation, we know from the previous chapter that attention and action are not only appropriate, but urgent. All parties—senior executives, the functional executives, and their wives—agree.

Selecting and Using the Appropriate Action Option

Once clear about the need to do something, you must choose among possible responses or "action options." Ten options are possible:

1.   *Include.* Increase the amount of diversity by adding a component or expanding the variability of the components in the mixture. Should the Tjax executives seek help from a

consultant who has diversity management skills, they would be doing both—increasing the number of components and adding variety to this mixture.

2. *Exclude.* Decrease the amount of diversity by reducing the number of components or the variability of the components in the mixture. Should Tjax's senior management conclude that one of the three functional executives is "the problem," they could practice exclusion. They might retain him but refuse to have him participate in future decision making. Or they might replace him with a more agreeable person.

3. *Deny.* Minimize the diversity mixture by explaining it away. If Tjax's senior management concludes that the challenges are "typical in this kind of situation" and decides to let the friends resolve the problems by themselves, management would be practicing denial.

4. *Isolate (Segregate).* Include and set "different" mixture components off to the side. The Tjax executives might decide to identify the decisions that cause them problems and set up a cross-functional department to deal with these situations. They may believe that developing "a department of integration specialists" will allow the functional heads to return to business as usual. This would be a classic case of isolation.

5. *Suppress.* Minimize mixture diversity by assigning it to the unconscious—beyond immediate awareness. Regardless of how the integration progresses, the Tjax friends agree not to discuss the "problem." Talking about the integration issue becomes absolutely off-limits both at work and at home. It becomes the "elephant in the room" that no one discusses.

6. *Assimilate.* Minimize mixture diversity by insisting that "minority" components not only conform to the norms of the dominant one, but commit to them. It is not enough just to go through the motions. If Tjax Company were to use this option, we would see consensus emerging as to which Tjax

function is dominant, and the heads of the other functions would defer to the thinking of that unit. They would understand the dominant view and genuinely believe it best for the company and the other functions.

7. *Acculturate.* Minimize mixture diversity by insisting that "minority" components conform to the norms of the dominant one, no matter how they feel about them. In this variation of assimilation, if the minority Tjax functions had conformed to the requirements of the dominant function but disagreed with them, they would have chosen acculturation—perhaps because it was the politically correct thing to do.

8. *Tolerate.* Adopt a room-for-all attitude, but keep interactions among mixture components superficial and limited. Here, Tjax's CEO will insist that the three functional heads be more open and accepting of each other's perspective. They respond by making a big "show" of soliciting each other's views and asking clarifying questions. However, neither their individual perspectives nor their ability to foster integration change. All perspectives are considered, but in a showy, superficial way.

9. *Build relationships.* Foster quality relationships, characterized by acceptance and understanding, among the mixture components. In response to the CEO's call for mutual understanding and acceptance, the three Tjax executives could convene a series of cross-functional meetings designed to explore, understand, and accept the others' differences, similarities, priorities, and requirements. These meetings bring progress toward mutual understanding and offer hope that this understanding will lead to greater integration.

10. *Foster mutual adaptation.* Expect all components to adapt to "requirements." Here, the goal is to identify where all components must conform (the requirements) and where they can be open to diversity (the nonrequirements). If they choose this option, the Tjax functional heads will build on the understanding achieved in their cross-functional meet-

ings and combine that capability with their assessments of requirements, both the corporation's and their own. They would use this information to construct a "requirements" platform on which to base integration decisions.

This last option—mutual adaptation–holds the most promise in the Tjax situation. That doesn't mean it is always the appropriate option. All of the action options are legitimate, and all are appropriate to the exact degree they facilitate fulfilling the mission, vision, strategy, and requirements of the specific situation. What's important is to learn how to choose the correct option or options—since combinations work well, too. Consider these examples of courses of action Tjax might elect:

- *Deny, suppress, and build relationships.* Believing that their friendships can overcome their integration problems, the three executives gather their families for a weekend retreat. During the retreat, they never mention any "integration issues." Instead, they reaffirm their long friendships and their commitment to maintain these relationships. They expect that this reaffirmation and recommitment will help them deal with managerial challenges at work.

- *Tolerate and suppress.* The executives work to be open to the views of each other's functions, while declaring a moratorium on any talk about integration problems.

- *Suppress and acculturate.* Over a period of four weeks, the three executives create a cultural web of suppression, where no one talks of integration challenges. None of the three really agrees with this "solution," but they go along for the sake of friendship and to maintain relative peace among the functions.

- *Include and assimilate/acculturate.* Tjax executives agree on a "solution" and insist that every new manager either genuinely concur with prevailing thinking or at least go along with it. These combinations are very common. The price of admission is conformity.

■ *Deny, assimilate/acculturate, and exclude.* Senior Tjax management concludes that the integration issue is overblown and threatens to fire any unit head or other functional manager who does not concur.

■ *Tolerate and foster mutual adaptation.* The Tjax executives identify "requirements" and agree to conform around them; they also decide to accept differences in the nonrequirements areas.

■ *Exclude and build relationships.* Senior Tjax management concludes that the three men have incompatible personalities. It then asks the three friends to complete a personality assessment instrument. The results reveal that the personality of one of the functional heads is not compatible with that of the other two. Senior executives fire him, recruit and hire a "compatible" replacement, and then require intensive team building for the new mixture of functional heads.

Every one of the options presented here is legitimate and realistic; Tjax could make a good case for choosing any of them. At issue is whether they are centered on the core requirement, which is to achieve the functional integration needed to exploit the company's new technology. Only those options that meet this end are valid.

DIVERSITY MATURITY

Diversity management skills are essential but not sufficient by themselves. They are effective only when joined with diversity maturity—experience, wisdom, and judgment.

People who are diversity mature are easy to recognize; they share several unique characteristics:

1. *They acknowledge being diversity challenged.* The Tjax executives cannot acknowledge this condition until they understand what it really means to be "diversity challenged." As long as they continue to operate from a politically correct

view of diversity, they are unlikely to see themselves as diversity challenged at all, since there are no racial, ethnic, and/or gender issues at the root of their problem. The three friends will probably have a difficult time achieving this aspect of diversity maturity.

2. *They recognize the costs of being diversity challenged.* In this case the costs are extreme, both professionally and personally. If the three men can acknowledge being diversity challenged, it will be relatively easy for them to see the costs of failure to achieve functional integration, and the threats to their health, friendships, and families.

3. *They accept diversity management responsibility.* With their positional authority, the Tjax friends will find it easy to accept responsibility for managing diversity, once they have acquired the first two characteristics. They will find it harder, I suspect, to determine how to go about it, especially if they lack a framework for approaching diversity issues.

4. *They know their own priorities and those of their organizations, and they are clear about SDM as a process.* The Tjax functional heads are clear about individual and organizational agendas. What they lack is operational knowledge about SDM. Attaining this knowledge will be key if the three executives are to forward.

5. *They act on the basis of requirements.* It is likely that the current functional preferences and traditions of the three friends may be incompatible with the company's new technology. For example, they have a preference for and tradition of relying on their friendship to cope with differences, but they'll need more than this to meet the integration challenge. They're likely to find it difficult to switch to making decisions based on requirements.

6. *They challenge conventional wisdom.* This capability, too, may be difficult for the Tjax friends, since they have spent

their careers in their respective silos. As they seek to exploit the new technology, they will have to challenge and go beyond past conventions.

7. *They engage in continuous learning.* The three friends will have to retool for new internal and external environments while preparing to pioneer new technology, at a time when similarly situated executives are resting on their laurels or applying hard-learned lessons from past successes. Their situation demonstrates that learning must be a continuous process. If they can't adapt, it will be difficult to achieve diversity maturity.

8. *They are comfortable with the dynamics of diversity.* The dynamic most difficult for the functional heads to come to terms with is the ongoing reality of diversity tension. If they are looking for a magic pill that will enhance their ability to make integrative decisions and thereby reduce, if not eliminate, the tension among the functions, they are going to be disappointed. Using the SDM craft would help them make better integrative decisions and would reduce the tension, but it would not eliminate it. Tension is integral to the situation. Tjax's CEO, the functional heads, and their families will have to become comfortable with this diversity dynamic.

Of all these characteristics, the first three—acknowledging that you are diversity challenged, recognizing that it has costs, and accepting diversity management responsibility—form the core of diversity maturity. All are hard to attain, and the first is probably the hardest of all. Yet acquiring them is a must. They form the base on which the remaining characteristics rest.

IN CONCLUSION . . .

Diversity management skills and diversity maturity are not niceties; they are essential foundations for mastering the craft of Strategic Diversity Management. Without them, you will not be able to use SDM. Without them, diversity management is like a car without an experienced driver. The vehicle of diversity management will remain in neutral and progress toward effective decision making in the midst of diversity will remain stalled.

CHAPTER

11

GETTING STARTED

_____

NO PROCESS, HOWEVER BENEFICIAL, is useful unless it can be applied. Succeeding or failing often boils down to a few tips—core ideas that have the ability to keep us focused, motivated, and creative. This chapter offers tips designed to ease novice SDM users through their first experience with the process. The tips should be equally useful in community, nonprofit, and for-profit settings.

Tip 1: Remember that the SDM craft is a capability. Using the process won't solve all of your diversity challenges. However, it will provide a path that allows you to generate solutions. These solutions won't resolve a specific diversity challenge forever, nor will they eliminate all present or future diversity challenges. But they will help you hone your craft. As you become more proficient at working through the challenges, it is less and less likely that the challenges you face will derail efforts to achieve your mission, vision, and strategy.

SDM can be compared to a good umbrella that allows you to reach your destination without becoming wet. Like rain showers, diversity challenges will keep coming, but SDM protects you over and over.

This tip is important because it will help you to avoid the unrealistic expectation that diversity challenges and diversity tension can be eliminated.

Tip 2: Keep the benefits of SDM firmly in mind. When using the craft for the first time, people describe the experience as "awkward," "laborious," and "tedious." Novice users often ask, "Why am I doing this?" SDM offers several potential benefits. The principal benefit is the ability to escape "the I-285 syndrome," or to avoid becoming stuck in the first place (see Chapter 5). The process:

■ *Provides quality maps.* SDM is grounded in clear concepts and fundamentals, as well as a user-friendly decision-making tool.

■ *Allows for multiple causation.* The concept of being "diversity challenged" acknowledges the "isms" (e.g., racism, sexism) and other potential causes (e.g., the complexity of the situation or cognitive limitations).

■ *Can be used by individuals, managers, and organizations.* SDM encourages individuals at all organizational ranks to take ownership of the process and become master craftspeople.

■ *Can be used alone or as a supplement to other perspectives.* In particular, the Strategic Diversity Management Process (SDMP) can be used, when desired, with frameworks built around the Civil Rights Movement.

■ *Can be applied universally.* SDM can be used with *any* mixture.

■ *Accommodates diversity tension.* SDM recognizes the reality of diversity tension and promotes quality decision making in its midst.

Tip 3: Keep the limitations of SDM in mind. SDM does not necessarily remove or minimize the causes of diversity tension, such as racism, sexism, or complexity. What it will do is help you function better in spite of that tension.

Tip 4: Use SDM universally to fully realize its potential. Limiting the application of SDM to people and workforce issues is like driving an automobile with a 400-horsepower engine at thirty-five miles per hour. It is an enormous waste of capability. In addition, by not using SDM in multiple arenas, you miss out on the economies and efficiencies of having one approach that can be used in many situations.

Tip 5: Choose an issue that is widely deemed worthy of attention for your initial SDM application. Doing so increases the likelihood that participants will be motivated and committed enough to work through the awkwardness, uncertainty, and inefficiencies that are inevitable at first. The most successful applications I've seen dealt with an issue that entailed both obvious pain and obvious opportunity for gain.

Tip 6: Remember to practice, practice, practice! Strategic Diversity Management is a craft, and mastery of it will require practice. If you don't practice, you will not achieve proficiency.

I am reminded here of my experience with golf. After ten years of planning to take up golfing, I finally made it to the driving range for lessons from a friend who agreed to introduce me to the game. After a frustrating episode of hacking, my friend stared in awe at my ineptness and said calmly, "I don't think you are going to get much better without some consistent practice."

Leaders who can only give a couple of hours for exposure and practice with SDM need to remember my friend's dismay. Be aware that your proficiency will mirror the amount of time committed. There is no substitute for practice. Without it, progress will be limited.

Tip 7: Work to minimize confusion between the paradigms of the Civil Rights Movement and SDM. It's difficult for novice SDM users, in particular, to avoid merging and confusing the two paradigms (see Figure 11-1, which outlines the significant differences between the two). The concepts and dynamics of the Civil Rights Movement are so much better known than those of SDM that it is easy to forget they are just one way of doing things. Without clarity, however, you won't be able to apply SDM effectively.

Tip 8: Recognize that SDM can complement the Civil Rights Movement paradigm. If they can distinguish between the two paradigms, leaders can come to understand that SDM does not compete with the Civil Rights Movement's vision of the Beloved Community, but rather can complement it. Specifically, it can facilitate integration on the basis of Dr. King's three ethical demands (see Chapter 3).

Stated differently, SDM can foster quality decision making around the ethical demands in the midst of the Beloved Community's racial differences, similarities, and tensions. This exposure, in turn, will foster greater receptivity for SDM and an openness to learn how it can be used for quality decision making with all kinds of diversity mixtures. The net result will be an enhanced ability to escape being stuck on diversity's I-285.

FIGURE 11-1

A tale of two paradigms: the "Beloved Community" and diversity management.

Variables	The Beloved Community	Strategic Diversity Management
Goals Critical Concepts	The Integrated Community • Racial Oppression • Equal Opportunity • Racial Segregation • Racial Desegregation • Racial Pluralism • Racial Integration • Racial Awareness and Sensitivity	Quality Decision Making • Diversity • Diversity Mixture • Diversity Challenges • Diversity Tensions • Diversity Skills • Diversity Maturity • Strategic Diversity Management Process
Facilitators of Integration	Dr. King's ethical demands: • We all are created by the same Creator. • Life demands freedom. • Everybody is somebody.	• Mission of Organization • Vision of Organization • Related Requirements
Current Status	Stuck on: • Racial Desegregation • Racial Pluralism	Stuck on: • Managing Workforce Representation • Understanding Workforce Relationships
Unfinished Business	• Racial Integration	• Managing Workforce Diversity • Managing Strategic Diversity Mixtures
Barriers	• Uneven Commitment to the Ethical Demands • Continuing Racism • The Challenge of Differences	• Allegiance to the Beloved Community Paradigm • Conceptual Confusion
Desired End	• All individuals are welcomed and enjoy spiritual unity and connectedness.	• Individual and organizational ability to make quality decisions in the midst of differences, similarities, and tensions.

PART FOUR

THE JOURNEY CONTINUES

CHAPTER

12

BECOMING A
DIVERSITY LEADER

I WROTE THIS BOOK BECAUSE I believe deeply that it matters whether we, individually and collectively, learn to manage diversity—or, in the language of this book, to make quality decisions in the midst of differences and similarities. The success of America's diversity experiment depends on it.

We cannot opt out of this experiment. Americans are a tremendously diverse people, and becoming more so. We must learn to work together on all levels if we are to achieve our common goals. Again, using the vocabulary of this book, the craft of diversity management must be mastered.

Yet the angry currents that now swirl around us—the intensity of the "cultural wars," the resegregation within our public schools, the proliferation of antidiscrimination lawsuits, the frequent failure of mergers and acquisitions, and the not uncommon inability of different functional units to work well together—all indicate that we have yet to learn how to do it.

Our ongoing inadequacies are not for lack of effort. Over the years, many have tried to address diversity, inspired by Martin Luther King's concept of "the Beloved Community," which is based on the ethical demands of mutual respect, freedom, and acknowledgment of humanity's oneness. We owe Dr. King an enduring debt of gratitude. Furthermore, the usefulness of his "ethical demands" is not limited to the past. They can provide a philosophical foundation for achieving cohesiveness and connectedness in the face of the various "cultural wars" that plague our country today.

So far, this foundation has not yet produced the hoped-for results. By itself, it could not be expected to do so. Dr. King was a visionary, and visionaries leave the details to others. He would have been the last person to suggest that his was the final word. To achieve Dr. King's integration vision, most individuals and groups need the impetus of a specific mission, vision, and strategy, and the capability provided by a structured process within which to work. Strategic Diversity Management (SDM) can provide that process, and in so doing it can serve to complement the agenda of the Civil Rights Movement. Dr. King's ethical demands can inform a variety of other initiatives as well.

As I say, it's not that we haven't tried. Business organizations have been particularly zealous. For years, all manner of interventions for minorities, ethnic groups, and women have been used and applauded. We have implemented outreach recruitment, developmental efforts, and retention practices. We have tried mentoring, changes in organizational culture, awareness training and education, and sensitivity training. Most of these efforts have been undertaken at considerable expense by committed, well-meaning people within enlightened organizations. Each of these initiatives can, in the right circumstances, be useful. But all have been part of the ongoing diversity cycle—a cycle so debilitating that some people argue that the very term *diversity* should be banished.

The term, however, is not the problem. The problem is that these initiatives have lacked the context that a structured process such as SDM provides. They represent, instead, specific manifestations of specific programs, what this book calls the "action options" (see Chapter 10), and thus by their very definition are limited in scope. Although decisions about these options are intrinsic to any diversity management efforts, they are insufficient to produce ongoing results.

THE PROMISE OF DIVERSITY

I believe that we can do better, and we must. That is why this book carries the title *Building on the Promise of Diversity*. I believe we can move to the next level in our workplaces, our communities, and our society.

Fulfilling the promise begins with the understanding that informed talk about diversity is not usually about differences and similarities per se, not about the specifics of what is and isn't different in any given situation. It is instead about taking action within the reality and challenges of diversity. That is, it is about diversity management—or, in the language of this book, making quality decisions in the midst of differences and similarities.

Fulfilling the promise also requires an understanding that the "promise" may be better understood as "potential." Diversity is neither intrinsically good nor bad. It can be a positive or negative force. Without competent diversity management, diversity's potential will be squandered.

The promise of diversity, then, is the potential it offers for a more fulfilling life. Those who learn to make quality decisions in the midst of diversity will be in a better position to achieve their mission and vision in the personal, organizational, and community arenas of their life. However, to do that, we must achieve the next level.

THE NEXT LEVEL WITH DIVERSITY

This next level will be achieved when diversity management efforts are informed and structured by the universal use of the specific craft of Strategic Diversity Management. When this happens, leaders will exchange the endless going-in-circles pattern of the I-285 syndrome for another pattern—a spiral moving constantly upward, a spiral characterized by continuing challenges and growth spurts in diversity management capability and achievement.

Achieving this next level will not, of course, eliminate all challenges and frustration. But when leaders are gaining skills and confidence in the SDM craft, frustrations are no longer fatal. Even when diversity efforts bring only limited progress, both the efforts themselves and their leaders will remain in a growth mode and avoid repeating the I-285 experience. They may have lost a battle, but they will retain the capabilities that give them the confidence to regroup and keep moving upward.

SDM: AN ESSENTIAL LIFE CRAFT

Like all essential life tasks, diversity management is too broad and too important to be left to the experts. Besides, it is not possible to do so, even if we might wish to.

The fact is that all of us, every single day, engage in diversity management, whether we know it or not. In every aspect of our lives, we are constantly faced with making quality decisions in situations that have both similarities and differences, and often tension as well. We cannot avoid diversity, so we had better become good at managing it. We need, in other words, to become masters at the craft of Strategic Diversity Management.

The significance of learning the SDM craft cannot be overstated. It might best be illustrated by its absence. Consider, for example, a golfer who aspires to "craftsperson" status but, because he refuses to take lessons, ends up annoying and frustrating his colleagues and himself. More damaging yet are those professionals who lack motivation to keep up with their craft but continue to practice. They place their unwary clients at considerable risk.

It behooves each of us, then, to become master SDM craftspeople. One way to begin is to observe the characteristics that all craftspeople share, regardless of their field of expertise.

Characteristics of Master Craftspeople

- They have developed competencies with their craft's concepts, fundamentals, methods, and tools.

- They recognize that they still have a lot to learn, no matter how long they have been active with the craft or how much recognition they have received.

- They respect their craft—even stand in awe of it. Given the opportunity, they launch spontaneously into an animated conversation about it. This awe and respect persist even if they experience serious frustration with the craft.

- They seek optimal familiarity with the craft. They know that while too little familiarity hampers competence, too much can generate arrogance or complacency. The true craftsperson desires a certain level of tension to ensure ongoing alertness for any challenges that might surface.

- They possess a realistic confidence in their capabilities, which enables them to admit readily that something is a challenge—and occasionally one that exceeds their capacities.

- They seek always to improve. They embrace challenges as opportunities for learning and further development of their craft capability.

- They are sanguine in the face of disappointing results. Such disappointments reinforce their respect for the craft and foster a realistic understanding of how much remains to be learned and mastered.

USING THE CRAFT TO MAKE A DIFFERENCE

I am convinced that competence in using the SDM process is a critical necessity—as opposed to "a nice thing to do." Diversity leaders who use SDM effectively and share the characteristics of master craftspeople will contribute substantially to their families, workplaces, and communities—indeed, to the nation as a whole. They also will have mastered one of life's essential tasks.

This book will have been a success if those who have read it embark on or continue their diversity management journey with a better understanding of its significance, a deeper knowledge of its requirements, a greater capability with the SDM framework, and—most of all—a sincere commitment to use this knowledge and those skills to benefit those people, organizations, and communities that matter to them most.

MASTERING THE BASICS

A CRITICAL STEP TOWARD DIVERSITY MATURITY—YOUR PERSONAL COACH

APPENDIX A:
A LETTER FROM THE AUTHOR

Dear Readers:

I have designed this instrument for individuals who wish to pursue diversity maturity by clarifying their understanding of the Strategic Diversity Management (SDM) Craft. This clarification is a critical foundation for attaining diversity maturity, which is, in turn, a requisite for becoming diversity capable.

Toward that end, this instrument will help you achieve the following objectives:

- Gain clarity about SDM.

- Sharpen your awareness of the differences and similarities between SDM and traditional thinking about diversity.

- Enhance your understanding of the SDM concepts and fundamentals—the heart of the craft.

- Foster your comprehension of SDM's thinking dynamics.

In addition to the objectives listed above, you can use the instrument on an ongoing basis to affirm and reinforce previous learning about SDM.

One individual's experience highlighted the need for this capability. Not long ago in a major Fortune 500 company, a senior executive attended three or four briefings I provided on SDM. When asked why he kept showing up, he replied, "This content is important, but just when I think I understand it, I lose it. And each time I hear the presentation, I learn something new."

For this executive and others similarly situated, I have designed this instrument to provide more than a one time benefit. It can be reviewed and, indeed, studied as often as needed in search of affirmations and new learning that will further your progress toward enhanced understanding and diversity maturity. This study can be done individually or in groups.

Mastering the Basics presents a set of common perceptions about diversity and for each perception asks that you indicate its consistency with SDM concepts and fundamentals. You should respond in the context of your understanding the SDM Basics. Then calculate your score and compare your responses to those offered as being most appropriate in the context of SDM. Rationales are provided for each recommendation.

I strongly urge you to view this tool not as a test but rather as a coach. Its purpose is **not to test you** on the SDM Basics but **to coach you** on them so that you can gain a deeper awareness, understanding, and working knowledge of the thinking dynamics (logic) behind the concepts, fundamentals, and their applications. This coaching is done through detailed rationales and specific guidelines for achieving a stronger grasp of SDM's concepts and fundamentals.

As a coaching tool, this instrument prescribes that you focus primarily on rationales, not on your score. By comparing the rationales for your responses to those for the recommended responses, you can determine where your thinking dynamics differ from those of the SDM concepts and fundamentals. Exploration of the rationales can highlight differing assumptions, interpretations, and nuances explicit and implicit in your rationales and those based on the SDM Basics and can also provide insight on how to achieve greater alignment with SDM.

Accordingly, I ask that you view your score as an indication of how different your diversity mindset is from that of the SDM concepts and fundamentals, not as a reflection of what was "right" or "wrong." The intent is that after completing this instrument and reviewing the rationales offered, you will have a sound grasp of the SDM Basics and how they can be applied in various settings.

I wish for you a great learning experience with this instrument (your coach).

Sincerely,

R. Roosevelt Thomas, Jr.

APPENDIX B: RESPONDING INSTRUCTIONS AND COMMON PERCEPTION RESPONSE ITEMS

THIRTY RESPONSE ITEMS appear on the next two pages. Read each statement and think carefully about whether it reflects "Very High" or "High" consistency with the Strategic Diversity Management (SDM) concepts and fundamentals, or "Very Low" or "Low" consistency with the SDM Basics. Take your time and make your selection. Then, circle the letter under your choice.

Example:	Consistency			
	Very High	High	Low	Very Low
Diversity is essentially about differences.	S	D	(M)	C

This instrument is intended neither to prescribe nor illustrate effective management of diversity, but rather to foster dialogue and comprehension of the Strategic Diversity Management Basics. Individuals seeking guidance concerning a specific diversity issue should consult a competent professional in the field.

Mastering the Basics: A Critical Step Toward Diversity Maturity—Your Personal Coach

Common Perception Response Items

Please indicate the extent to which you think that each "common perception" is consistent with SDM Basics (concepts and fundamentals).	Consistency			
	Very High	High	Low	Very Low
		(Please circle one)		
1. Diversity is America's strength.	S	D	M	C
2. For most organizations, the issue of race is a critical aspect of diversity.	S	D	C	M
3. Diversity is primarily about focusing on our similarities (commonalities).	S	D	M	C
4. Diversity is about being inclusive.	S	D	M	C
5. In the United States, racial diversity issues cause much more "heat" than other diversity topics.	S	D	C	M
6. Harmony is the goal of diversity management.	S	D	M	C
7. Unity is the goal of diversity management.	M	C	D	S
8. Getting rid of the "isms" (racism, sexism, etc.) helps achieve effective diversity management.	M	C	D	S
9. Racial tension in the workplace is caused by racism.	S	D	M	C
10. Diversity is the "right" thing to do.	M	C	D	S
11. Effective management of diversity results in "fairness."	M	C	D	S

12. The "Golden Rule" (do unto others as you would have them do unto you) captures the essence of diversity.	S	D	M	C
13. Diversity as a field of study and practice dates back to the Civil Rights Movement in the 1960s.	S	D	M	C
14. By far, race is the most challenging aspect of workforce diversity.	S	D	C	M
15. Effective diversity management recommends that everyone be treated the same.	S	D	C	M
16. Assimilation (when a minority person or group seeks to be like the majority) calls for conformity and therefore conflicts with effective diversity management.	S	D	M	C
17. African-Americans do not require diversity training, because they live diversity daily.	S	D	M	C
18. Theories, concepts, and fundamentals are not needed. We've had too much talk. Now we need effective, concrete, action steps—more than ever!	S	D	M	C
19. When individuals achieve effectiveness with family diversity issues, few—if any—benefits flow to the corporation with respect to workforce diversity.	S	D	M	C
20. When there is effective diversity management, there is less racial tension.	S	D	C	M
21. To focus on diversity mixtures other than race, gender, and ethnicity distracts from the attention that should be given to these traditional issues.	S	D	M	C

22. A racist and/or sexist manager cannot be effective in managing racial and gender diversity.	S	D	M	C
23. Unless women and minorities are well represented, a workplace cannot be considered very diverse.	S	D	M	C
24. Effective management of employee diversity does not eliminate the need to conform to the cultural norms of the organization.	M	C	D	S
25. Efforts to accept and value minorities and women are critical to the effective management of workforce diversity.	M	C	D	S
26. The CEO is key to establishing effective diversity management in a corporation.	M	C	D	S
27. Although we can speak of mergers and an organization's functions as diversity mixtures, for most corporations, this "diversity" is not as important as racial and gender diversity.	S	D	C	M
28. At its core, effective diversity management is about getting rid of racism, sexism, and other "isms."	S	D	M	C
29. Although a collection of a corporation's brands or products may represent a diversity mixture, its dynamics are very different from those of racial and gender diversity in the workforce.	S	D	C	M
30. Effective diversity management requires that an organization reduce its use of affirmative action In favor of more advanced practices.	S	D	C	M

APPENDIX C:
TALLYING, SCORING, AND INTERPRETING SCORES

Tallying and Scoring Guidelines

1. Return to Appendix B and total the "S" responses and put that number on the "S" line in the Count column of the Tally Box.

2. Repeat the same procedure for the "D," "M," and "C" responses, and put those totals on their respective lines in the Tally Box's Count column.

3. Multiply the total for "S" by the Factor in the Tally Box and put the answer in the Product column on the "S" row.

4. Repeat the same procedure for the "D," "M," and "C" rows.

5. Add the four answers in the Product column together and record the grand total in the "SDMC Score" box.

6. On the following five pages you will find the "Interpreting Your Score" section. Locate the range your score falls in and place your score in the box on the first page.

Tally Box		
Count	**Factor**	**Product**
S _____	× 1	=
D _____	× 2	=
M _____	× 3	=
C _____	× 4	=
YOUR SDMC SCORE _____		

Interpreting Your Score

SDMC Score
_____

If you scored 105–120

Your score indicates that at the introductory level, you possess an excellent feel for the thinking dynamics of the Strategic Diversity Management Craft's Basics (concepts and fundamentals) and their implications. In preparation for moving further toward diversity maturity, should you desire, I recommend that you consider building on your grasp of the Basics by pursuing greater capability with one of the other diversity maturity characteristics, such as knowing your own priorities (mission, vision and strategy), acknowledging that you are diversity challenged, and recognizing the costs of your being diversity challenged.

■ *Knowing your own priorities (mission, vision, and strategy).* Here, the key questions for you to answer are:

- What is my mission? (What is my purpose? What's really important to me?)
- What is my vision? (If I were able to achieve my mission, what would be the characteristics of my success?) People with clear visions easily describe the future in terms of the manifestations of realizing their mission.
- What strategic steps will be required to achieve my mission and vision?
- What requirements (as opposed to preferences, traditions, or conveniences) must be fulfilled if my strategy is to be executed and my mission and vision realized?

Maturity and awareness along these **personal** lines are essential as context for quality decision making in the midst of diversity.

■ *Acknowledging that you are diversity challenged.* This is a critical aspect of achieving diversity maturity. Without this awareness, your motivation for pursuing enhanced diversity capability declines.

You might seek out three or four people who know you well in different settings, such as your workplace, family, and a community organization. Explain to them the concept of being diversity challenged. Once convinced that they understand the notion, ask them candidly to share their perceptions of how you are diversity challenged. Take care to stress your desire for their honest and objective opinions.

As you receive their views, keep in mind your expressed desire for candor and avoid becoming defensive. Feedback from three or four individuals should give you a good sense of how and where you are diversity challenged.

■ *Recognizing the costs of your being diversity challenged.* Two indicators that being diversity challenged in a particular manner may be costly are the enthusiasm and confidence of the reporting individuals as they convey their perceptions, and also the degree of discomfort you experience on hearing the perceived challenge. If an acquaintance feels strongly about one of your challenges, it very well may be hampering your relationship with this person, and if you value that relationship, the costs for you may be significant. Similarly, if you are uncomfortable hearing the report of the challenge, a strong likelihood exists that there may be substantial related costs. My experience has been that the greater the discomfort, the greater the related costs. You would do well to ferret out these costs and to understand them.

A second way of identifying costs is to determine how a particular way in which you are reportedly diversity challenged relates to your personal mission, vision, strategy, and requirements. To the extent that the challenge in question is not compatible with your personal priorities, it can be very costly. You want to forthrightly recognize these challenges and their costs, so that you might determine how to minimize their impact.

If you scored 90–104

Your score indicates that at the introductory level, you have a solid grasp of the SDM Basics (concepts and fundamentals) and their implications. In preparation for moving to the next level, should you desire, I recommend that you consider the following:

- Review the results from your completion of the "A Task for Readers" at the conclusion of Chapter 6. If you did not complete this task, I recommend that you do so at this point.

- Compare the results of your analysis from the Chapter 6 task assignment to the SDM concepts and fundamentals. Look for key differences and similarities.

- For about a two-week period, log "diversity experiences you encounter." For some of the most critical ones, compare how you handled them to the actions SDM Basics would have pre-scribed. Determine which differences between your mindset and the thinking dynamics of SDM concepts and fundamentals contributed to the gap (if any) between the actions you took and those called for by the Basics.

■ Review the rationales offered in the instrument, especially for items where your responses differed markedly from those recommended. Determine how the differences between your perspective and the SDM Basics may have influenced your responses.

■ Request a copy of the instrument and retake it.

If you scored 89 or less

Your score reflects that you are in the early stages of becoming familiar with the thinking dynamics of the SDM Basics (concepts and fundamentals). Again, I urge you to view your score as an indication of the differences between your diversity mindset and that of the Basics. Remember, SDM concepts and fundamentals represent a way of thinking about diversity-related issues. In this light, your score indicates that your thinking dynamics about diversity differ significantly from the logic of the SDM Basics.

Your reaction should not be, "Good grief! I really blew this test!" but rather, "This is interesting. What assumptions, interpretations, and nuances differentiate the logic of the Basics from my way of thinking?" Obviously, this latter approach goes against the grain of achievement-oriented, competitive individuals accustomed to doing well on "tests."

This is not a test. This instrument primarily provides coaching for individuals desiring deeper learning regarding SDM concepts and fundamentals. The approach recommended above likely will allow you the greatest realization of the tool's coaching potential. In preparation for moving to the next level, should you desire, you should consider the following:

■   Reread Chapters 7, 8, and 9.

■   Review the results from your completion of "A Task for Read-
     ers" at the conclusion of Chapter 6. If you did not complete
     this task, I recommend that you do so at this point.

■   Compare the results of your analysis from the Chapter 6 task
     assignment to the SDM concepts and fundamentals. Look for
     key differences and similarities.

■   Review the rationales offered in the instrument, especially for
     items where your responses differed markedly from those rec-
     ommended. Determine how the differences between your
     perspective and the SDM Basics may have influenced your
     responses.

■   Request a copy of the instrument and retake it.

Rationales and Interpretations

A list of the SDM concepts and fundamentals can be found on pages 206 and 207.

1. A Common Perception: Diversity is America's strength.

Strategic Diversity Management (SDM) Basics Response: "Very Low Consistency."

Rationale: While diversity **can** be a strength, ***SDM Fundamental 2*** posits that diversity in and of itself is neither a weakness nor a strength. It is simply a reality. In a particular situation, diversity can be positive, negative, or neutral in impact. What determines impact is how diversity is managed. Therefore, effective diversity **management** can be an enormous strength for a country or an organization—more so than just the presence of diversity.

Also, ***SDM Concept 1*** suggests that in a given situation, the nature of the impact can depend on the type of diversity in question.

195

2. A Common Perception: For most organizations, the issue of race is a critical aspect of diversity.

SDM Basics Response: "Low Consistency."

Rationale: In most organizations, people are concerned about racial diversity. However, this does not necessarily mean that race is a critical aspect of diversity for these enterprises. Other diversity issues may be more urgent for a given enterprise. Often, diversity related to gender, ethnicity, mergers, buyouts, and global concerns is more critical. It is rare that racial or any other type of diversity is "critical" to all organizations. Key determinants of whether a particular type of diversity is critical are an organization's external environment, mission, vision, and strategy. (See ***Concept 1*** and ***Fundamental 2***.)

3. A Common Perception: Diversity is primarily about focusing on our similarities (commonalities).

SDM Basics Response: "Very Low Consistency."

Rationale: ***Concept 1*** defines diversity as the mix of differences, similarities, **and** tensions that can exist among the elements of a collective mixture.

A diverse mixture contains more than one variety of something. For example, within a racially diverse workforce, we find both differences and similarities (including differences and similarities in attributes) among those representing different racial groups. Possible attributes along which there could be differences and similarities— other than race—would be age, gender, place of birth, length of service with the organization, and sexual orientation.

4. A Common Perception: Diversity is about being inclusive.

SDM Basics Response: "Very Low Consistency."

Rationale: Effective diversity management is as much about exclusion as it is about inclusion. Both options can be an appropriate response to certain dimensions of diversity within a given situation. (See *Fundamental 2*.)

5. A Common Perception: In the United States, racial diversity issues cause much greater "heat" than any other diversity topics.

SDM Basics Response: "Low Consistency."

Rationale: Many diverse mixtures can cause intense "heat." For instance, in some circumstances, mixtures that consist of elements such as age, gender, sexual orientation, religion, and immigration status may cause more "heat" than mixtures relating to race. (See *Fundamental 2*.)

6. A Common Perception: Harmony is the goal of diversity management.

SDM Basics Response: "Very Low Consistency."

Rationale: Harmony is not the goal of diversity management. A diverse mixture of people may have harmony yet still be unable to reach decisions around shared objectives. Conversely, a group can lack harmony and still succeed in achieving its aspirations. The goal of diversity management is to advance organizational and personal objectives through quality (requirements-driven) decisions. (See *Fundamentals 3* and *4*.)

Concept 2 states that "Strategic Diversity Management is a craft for enhancing the way people make quality decisions in situations where there are critical differences, similarities, and *tensions*."

7. A Common Perception: Unity is the goal of diversity management.

SDM Basics Response: "High Consistency."

Rationale: Unity of *purpose* is essential to effective diversity management and can exist even where there is a lack of harmony. (See *Concept 2* and *Fundamental 3*.)

8. A Common Perception: Getting rid of the "isms" (racism, sexism, etc.) helps achieve effective diversity management.

SDM Basics Response: "High Consistency."

Rationale: Getting rid of the "isms" **may** help bring about effective diversity management. However, that alone may neither be necessary nor enough. In other words, it is possible to manage diversity effectively without getting rid of the "isms." It also is possible to eliminate the "isms" without making progress toward effective diversity management. (See *Concepts 2* and *4* and *Fundamental 3*.)

9. A Common Perception: Racial tension in the workplace is caused by racism.

SDM Basics Response: "Very Low Consistency."

Rationale: Racism is only one possible cause of "racist" behavior. For example, "racist" behavior can be caused by the lack of familiarity with a particular racial group. It may also be caused by the complexity and challenges that come about when people of many races come together.

Regardless of whether racism is present, if there is racial diversity, there will be racial tension. The challenge is to make quality decisions in the midst of racial differences, similarities, and tensions. (See *Concepts 2*, *3*, and *4*.)

10. A Common Perception: Diversity is the "right" thing to do.

SDM Basics Response: "High Consistency."

Rationale: If "right" relates to an important business reason, this statement is in agreement with SDM Basics. However, if "right" solely means doing what is morally, legally, or socially correct, this statement minimizes the importance of being "requirements driven" for effective diversity management. (See *Fundamentals 2* and *3*.)

11. A Common Perception: Effective management of diversity results in "fairness."

SDM Basics Response: "High Consistency."

Rationale: Ideally, effective diversity management will result in "fairness." That's because quality decisions will be made on the basis of requirements, which are applied equally across the board. (See **Fundamental 3**.) Although fairness is not the sole purpose of effective diversity management, its effort to foster achievement of individual and organizational objectives can have this impact. (See **Concept 2** and **Fundamental 4**.) Purpose and potential impact differ.

12. A Common Perception: The "Golden Rule" (do unto others as you would have them do unto you) captures the essence of diversity.

SDM Basics Response: "Very Low Consistency."

Rationale: The "Golden Rule" only works in dealing with diversity if everyone wishes to be treated the same as you wish to be treated. This approach ignores the unique expectations and ways of interacting that make up a diverse population. The essence of SDM is quality decision making—the context for which is an organization's mission, vision, and strategy, rather than the individual's interpretation or application of the "Golden Rule." (See **Concept 2** and **Fundamental 3**.)

13. A Common Perception: Diversity as a field of study and practice dates back to the Civil Rights Movement in the 1960s.

SDM Basics Response: "Very Low Consistency."

Rationale: The concept of "diversity" dates back to the late 1960s. At that time, diversity was mostly used to describe business activities. It referred to different functions, products, or lines of business and how they related to the larger corporation. However, by the mid-1980s, use of the concept evolved to cover "people" diversity in the workforce and in organizations, and it became an important field of study and practice.

In the 1960s, when managers sought to increase the number of minorities and women in the workforce in conjunction with the Civil Rights Movement, the motive was demographic representation (inclusion) as a means of overcoming or compensating for past practices of discrimination. These managers were not seeking *diversity* or the potential benefits that could be gained through effective diversity management. Stated differently, the goals of Strategic Diversity Management are compatible with, but different from, those of the Civil Rights Movement. (See *Concepts 1* and *2*.)

14. A Common Perception: By far, race is the most challenging aspect of workforce diversity.

SDM Basics Response: "Low Consistency."

Rationale: Members of the workforce can be diverse (different and similar) in a number of ways such as race, gender, religion, background, national origin, and sexual orientation. In many settings, race is not the most challenging diversity issue. For example, in some corporations, gender, sexual orientation, religion, and/or age can be more challenging. Also, workplace issues such as mergers and buyouts can create more challenges than workforce concerns in general. (See *Concept 1* and *Fundamentals 2* and *3*.)

15. A Common Perception: Effective diversity management recommends that everyone be treated the same.

SDM Basics Response: "Low Consistency."

Rationale: Effective diversity management implies that people should be treated equitably, which **can** mean treating different people differently. This is why it is critical to make decisions based on requirements. (See *Concept 2* and *Fundamental 3*.)

16. A Common Perception: Assimilation (when a minority person or group seeks to be like the majority) calls for conformity and therefore conflicts with effective diversity management.

SDM Basics Response: "Very Low Consistency."

Rationale: Assimilation is one of several responses to diversity that can be perfectly appropriate under certain circumstances. If the assimilation is in response to a "requirement," there is absolutely no room for diversity. It is in the area of nonrequirements that diversity can exist and thrive. (See ***Fundamental 3***.)

17. A Common Perception: African-Americans do not require diversity training, because they live diversity daily.

SDM Basics Response: "Very Low Consistency."

Rationale: This statement presumes that diversity management is about eliminating racism, and that since African-Americans have been victimized by racism, they have a sensitivity that enables them to avoid being racist. However, since diversity management is not about the elimination of racism, but rather quality decision making in the midst of **any** mixture of differences, similarities and tensions, no basis exists for assuming African-Americans are better prepared than others to manage diversity. (See ***Concepts 1*** and ***2***.)

18. A Common Perception: Theories, concepts, and fundamentals are not needed. We've had too much talk. Now we need effective, concrete action steps—more than ever!

SDM Basics Response: "Very Low Consistency."

Rationale: The craft of Strategic Diversity Management dictates that concepts, fundamentals, **and** action steps are equally important. Concepts and fundamentals provide a contextual grounding for the development and implementation of action steps. Further, the fundamentals suggest that the decision making generated by use of the SDM craft focuses on action steps that support the concrete—mission, vision, strategy, and requirements—rather than actions that are focused solely on either increasing demographic diversity or learning to get along. (See *Concepts 2*, *3*, and *5*, and *Fundamentals 2* and *3*.)

19. A Common Perception: When individuals achieve effectiveness with family diversity issues, few—if any—learnings can be applied to workforce diversity—since these types of diversity differ significantly.

SDM Basics Response: "Very Low Consistency."

Rationale: A basic premise of the craft of SDM is that it can be applied to all types of diversity management challenges. (See *Concepts 1* and *2* and *Fundamental 5*.)

20. A Common Perception: When there is effective diversity management, there is less racial tension.

SDM Basics Response: "Low Consistency."

Rationale: Effective management of racial diversity **can** reduce racial tension but not always. Remember: If there is diversity, there will be diversity tension. Progress in managing racial diversity does not always reduce racial tension. Reducing racial tension is not the goal of SDM. What progress in managing racial diversity will do is enable one to work through the tension more effectively to achieve better outcomes. (See *Concepts 2* and *3*.)

21. A Common Perception: To focus on diversity mixtures other than race, gender, and ethnicity detracts from the attention that these traditional issues require.

SDM Basics Response: "Very Low Consistency."

Rationale: Focusing on the mixtures that are **most critical** to the success of the organization will always ensure the right level of attention to the right mixtures. Although race and gender may not make the top of the critical list in a given organization, one can be certain that everyone becomes more skillful in addressing race, gender, and ethnic diversity as he or she strengthens his or her capability to use the craft in other arenas. (See ***Fundamentals 2*** and ***5***.)

22. A Common Perception: A racist and/or sexist manager cannot be effective in managing racial and gender diversity.

SDM Basics Response: "Very Low Consistency."

Rationale: One can be effective in managing diversity even if he or she is a racist or a sexist. The basis for this statement is that being diversity capable means that one can make quality decisions in the midst of differences, similarities, and tensions. People can, and do, behave contrary to their personal beliefs if given the right incentives. In organizations that are requirements driven, even individuals who suffer from "isms" can exhibit the appropriate level of diversity maturity to be effective in managing racial or gender diversity. (See ***Concepts 2*** and ***5*** and ***Fundamental 3***.)

23. A Common Perception: Unless women and minorities are well represented, a workplace cannot be considered very diverse.

SDM Basics Response: "Very Low Consistency."

Rationale: Workforce diversity can exist in a variety of ways—not just race and gender; for example, age, sexual orientation, educational background, and geographic origin. Further, an organization can lack workforce demographic diversity and yet have other kinds of diversity, such as functional, product, customer, and acquisition/merger diversity. (See ***Concept 1***.)

24. A Common Perception: Effective management of employee diversity does not eliminate the need to conform to the cultural norms of the organization.

SDM Basics Response: "High Consistency."

Rationale: This statement is in agreement with the SDM Basics as long as the cultural "norms" are absolute requirements for achieving the organization's mission and vision. Although requirements for conformity may seem contrary to diversity management, keep in mind that within the realm of requirements we must conform. It is only outside of requirements (around nonrequirements) that there is room for diversity. (See *Fundamental 3*.)

25. A Common Perception: Efforts to accept and value minorities and women are critical to the effective management of workforce diversity.

SDM Basics Response: "High Consistency."

Rationale: Accepting minorities and women is a critical aspect of the effective management of workforce diversity. However, how we value them is related to the quality of the contribution they bring to the workplace.

To accept minorities and women is to acknowledge them as being as capable as any other group of making important contributions to the achievement of organizational "requirements." All individuals or groups who make such contributions should be valued. However, there is nothing inherent in the craft of SDM dictating that minorities or women, or any other individual or group in the organization, should be valued in the absence of quality contributions. (See *Fundamentals 2* and *3*.)

26. A Common Perception: The CEO is key to establishing effective diversity management in a corporation.

SDM Basics Response: "High Consistency."

Rationale: SDM concepts and fundamentals suggest that CEO endorsement can be key to successful implementation. Endorsement means the CEO models being diversity capable and also effectively pushes the organization toward that end. This reflects the reality that it is equally important (key) for **all** managers and associates to also be diversity capable. (See *Concept 5* and *Fundamental 4*.)

27. A Common Perception: Although we can speak of mergers and an organization's functions as diversity mixtures, for most corporations, this "diversity" is not as important as racial and gender diversity.

SDM Basics Response: "Low Consistency."

Rationale: SDM Basics recognize the possibility that diversity in areas other than race and gender can be the most important for a particular organization. Indeed, this is often the case. (See *Concept 1* and *Fundamentals 2*, *3*, and *5*.)

28. A Common Perception: At its core, effective diversity management is about getting rid of racism, sexism, and other "isms."

SDM Basics Response: "Very Low Consistency."

Rationale: Getting rid of racism, sexism, and other "isms" is not the objective of effective diversity management although it may be a result. The objective is to make quality decisions that foster the objectives of the organization regardless of whether racism, sexism, and other "isms" are present. (See *Concept 2* and *Fundamentals 2* and *3*.)

29. A Common Perception: Although a collection of a corporation's brands or products may represent a diversity mixture, its dynamics are very different from those of racial and gender diversity in the workforce.

SDM Basics Response: "Low Consistency."

Rationale: A basic premise of the craft of SDM is that all diversity mixtures experience the dynamics generated by similarities, differences, and their related tensions. Because effective diversity management relates to the ability to handle any diversity mixture, addressing these mixtures calls for the same capabilities as those required by racial or gender diversity.

(See *Concepts 1*, *2*, and *3* and *Fundamental 5*.)

30. A Common Perception: Effective diversity management requires that an organization reduce its use of affirmative action in favor of more advanced practices.

SDM Basics Response: "Low Consistency."

Rationale: Effective diversity management does not call for a reduction in affirmative action. Rather, it builds upon affirmative action as one way to create a demographically representative workforce. Having representation goals is an appropriate option. However, to access the talent of a representative workforce, the organization's leadership must have diversity management capability. (See *Concepts 1* and *2* and *Fundamentals 2* and *3*.)

Five SDM Undergirding Concepts

1. Diversity is the mix of differences, similarities, and tensions that can exist among the elements of a collective mixture.

2. Strategic Diversity Management is a craft for enhancing the way people make quality decisions in situations where there are critical differences, similarities, and tensions.

3. Diversity tension is the stress, strain, and anxiety that tend to flow from the interaction of differences and similarities.

4. Diversity challenged means that an individual or organization has difficulty making quality decisions when differences, similarities, and tensions exist.

5. Diversity capable means that an individual or organization has mastered the craft of making quality decisions in spite of differences, similarities, and related tensions. One may be diversity capable along one dimension, while remaining diversity challenged along other diversity dimensions.

Five SDM Fundamentals

1. Before decision making begins, there must first be a shared understanding of the core diversity management concepts.

2. Context (environment, mission, vision, and strategy) is a key consideration for quality decision making in the midst of differences, similarities, and tensions.

3. Being requirements driven is critical, as opposed to basing decisions on personal preferences, traditions, or conveniences.

4. The diversity aspirations of both individuals **and** their enterprises must be considered if quality diversity management decisions are to be made.

5. To manage diversity effectively, enterprises and individuals must apply the SDM craft universally—with **any** mixture that is critical.

CHAPTER 1—DIVERSITY: IN SEARCH OF THE NEXT LEVEL

1. John W. Gardner, *Living, Leading, and the American Dream* (San Francisco: Jossey-Bass, 2003), p. 182.

2. Ibid., p. 182; and Arthur M. Schlesinger, Jr., *The Disuniting of America* (New York: W. W. Norton & Company, 1992), p. 129.

3. Mickey Connolly and Richard Rianoshek, *The Communication Catalyst: The Fast (But Not Stupid) Track to Value for Customers, Investors, and Employees* (Chicago: Dearborn Trade Publishing, 2002), pp. 38–39.

4. R. Roosevelt Thomas, Jr., *Building a House for Diversity: How a Fable About a Giraffe & an Elephant Offers New Strategies for Today's Workforce* (New York: AMACOM, 1999), pp. 25–52.

5. Connolly and Rianoshek, *The Communication Catalyst,* p. 39.

CHAPTER 2—THE UNITED STATES: AN EXPERIMENT IN DIVERSITY

1. Nathan Glazer, *Affirmative Discrimination: Ethnic Inequality and Public Policy* (New York: Basic Books, 1975), p. 7.

2. Arthur M. Schlesinger, Jr., *The Disuniting of America* (New York: W. W. Norton & Company, 1992), p. 129.

3. Ibid., pp. 129–130.

4. Glazer, *Affirmative Discrimination*, pp. 5, 8–32.

5. Ibid., pp. 5, 8.

6. Ibid., p. 5.

7. Ibid.

8. Benjamin Schwarz, "The Diversity Myth: America's Leading Export," *Atlantic Monthly* (May 1995), p. 2.

9. Peter Brimelow, *Alien Nation: Common Sense About America's Immigration Disaster* (New York: Random House, 1995), p. 10.

10. Ibid., p. 17.

11. Schlesinger, *The Disuniting of America,* p. 138.

12. Samuel P. Huntington, *Who Are We? The Challenges to America's National Identity* (New York: Simon & Schuster, 2004), p. 9.

13. John W. Gardner, *Living, Leading, and the American Dream* (San Francisco: Jossey-Bass, 2003), p. 182.

14. Schlesinger, *The Disuniting of America,* p. 15.

15. Nathan Glazer, *We Are All Multiculturalists Now* (Cambridge, MA: Harvard University Press), pp. 11, 120, 159.

16. Glazer, *We Are All Multiculturalists Now,* p. 20.

17. Huntington, *Who Are We?* p. 40.

18. Schlesinger, *The Disuniting of America,* p. 15.

19. Glazer, *We Are All Multiculturalists Now,* pp. 11, 96–97. Glazer's definition of multiculturalism explicitly and implicitly endorses assimilation that is less Anglo-centric in nature.

20. Ibid., pp. 97–98.

21. Gardner, *Living, Leading, and the American Dream,* p. 182.

22. Ibid.

23. Huntington, *Who Are We?* pp. 362–366.

24. Ibid., pp. 20, 365–366.

25. Ibid., pp. xvii, 30.

26. Schlesinger, *The Disuniting of America,* p. 135.

27. Glazer, *We Are All Multiculturalists Now,* p. 159.

28. Huntington, *Who Are We?* pp. 315, 340.

CHAPTER 3—THE CIVIL RIGHTS MOVEMENT: IN PURSUIT OF THE "BELOVED COMMUNITY"

1. Walter E. Fluker, *They Looked for a City: A Comparative Analysis of Community in the Thought of Howard Thurman and Martin Luther King, Jr.* (Lanham, MD: University Press of America, 1989), pp. 110–111. Fluker, a professor at Morehouse College and an authority on leadership, attributes the term *Beloved Community* to Josiah Royce and R. H. Lotze—two pioneers in the development of the philosophy of "personal idealism." Particularly, Royce saw the Beloved Community as a "solidaritic view" of human society. Dr. King evolved this concept into a code or symbol for his highest aspirations for the nation with respect to racial desegregation, pluralism, and integration.

2. Clayborne Carson, *Civil Rights Chronicle* (Lincolnwood, IL: Legacy Publishing, 2003), p. 35.

3. Ibid., p. 37.

4. Tamar Jacoby, *Someone Else's House: America's Unfinished Struggle for Integration* (New York: The Free Press, 1998), p. 39.

5. Ibid., p. 39.

6. Ibid., pp. 42–45.

7. Michael Eric Dyson, *I May Not Get There with You: The True Story of Martin Luther King, Jr.* (New York: The Free Press, 2000), p. 116.

8. Jacoby, *Someone Else's House*, p. 45.

9. Carson, *Civil Rights Chronicle*, p. 120.

10. Jacoby, *Someone Else's House*, p. 35.

11. Martin Luther King, Jr., "The Ethical Demands for Integration," in *A Testament of Hope: The Essential Writings of Martin Luther King, Jr.*, ed. James M. Washington (San Francisco: Harper & Row, 1986), pp. 117–125.

12. Ibid., p. 118.

13. Ibid., pp. 118, 124.

14. Ibid., pp. 118–122.

15. Ibid., p. 122.

16. Fredrik Sunnemark, *Ring Out Freedom! The Voice of Martin*

Luther King, Jr. and the Making of the Civil Rights Movement (Bloomington: Indiana University Press, 2004), p. 71.

17. Ibid., pp. 72–73.

18. Martin Luther King, Jr., "The American Dream," in *A Testament of Hope*, pp. 208–209.

19. Jacoby, *Someone Else's House*, pp. 3, 34, 37–38.

20. Dyson, *I May Not Get There with You*, p. 39.

CHAPTER 4—DIVERSITY AND AFFIRMATIVE ACTION: PAST, PRESENT, AND FUTURE

1. Opinion of the Court, Supreme Court of the United States, No. 02-241, Barbara Grutter, *Petitioner* v. *Lee Bollinger et al.*, June 23, 2003, p. 30.

2. Ibid., p. 31.

3. "Statute Summary: Executive Order 11246," accessed through http://www.elinfonet.com/11246sum.php.

4. Nathan Glazer, *Affirmative Discrimination: Ethnic Inequality and Public Policy* (New York: Basic Books, 1975), pp. 45–49. In these pages, Glazer provides a history of the executive orders through 1965 that gave rise to affirmative action and of the early guidelines that followed.

5. Ibid., pp. 4, 44.

6. John W. Gardner, *Excellence* (New York: W. W. Norton & Company, 1984), pp. 43–44; and Stephen Steinberg, *Turning Back: The Retreat from Racial Justice in American Thought and Policy* (Boston: Beacon, 1995), p. 165.

7. Arch Puddington, "What to Do About Affirmative Action," *Commentary* (June 1995), p. 23; and Steinberg, *Turning Back*, pp. 165–166. Puddington offers a concise discussion of how some change advocates came to see "institutional racism" as a major barrier to progress. Steinberg distinguishes between "outreach" affirmative action and "racial preferences" affirmative action, arguing that the latter

was a last resort against "entrenched patterns of racial and gender segregation."

8. Gardner, *Excellence,* p. 43.

9. Glazer, *Affirmative Discrimination*, pp. 4, 44–45.

10. Paul Craig Roberts and Lawrence M. Stratton, "Color Code," *National Review* (March 20, 1995), p. 36.

11. Gardner, *Excellence*, p. 47.

12. Ibid., p. 48.

13. Ibid., p. 49.

14. Roger Wilkins, "Racism Has Its Privileges: The Case for Affirmative Action," *The Nation* (March 27, 1995), p. 410. Wilkins argues the compensatory case.

15. Raymond A. Winbush, ed., *Should America Pay? Slavery and the Raging Debate on Reparations* (New York: Amistad, an imprint of HarperCollins Publishing, 2003). This book contains a comprehensive set of articles on the topic of reparations.

16. Max Frankel, "Reaffirm the Affirmative," *New York Times Magazine* (February 26, 1995), p. 22.

17. Glazer, *Affirmative Discrimination*, p. 31.

18. Wilkins, "Racism Has Its Privileges," p. 412.

19. Jeffrey Rosen, "The Color Blind Court," *The New Republic* (July 31, 1995), pp. 19–25.

20. Glazer, *Affirmative Discrimination*, p. 31.

21. Stephen L. Carter, *Reflections of an Affirmative Action Baby* (New York: Basic Books, 1991), pp. 47–50.

CHAPTER 5—CURRENT STATUS OF THE DIVERSITY FIELD: JUST PLAIN STUCK

1. R. Roosevelt Thomas, Jr., *Beyond Race and Gender: Unleashing the Power of Your Total Workforce by Managing Diversity* (New York: AMACOM, 1991), p. 21.

2. Jim Wooten, "Our Opinion: Democratic Coup Under Gold Dome," *The Atlanta Journal Constitution* (September 2, 2001), p. D8.

3. Thomas Sowell, *Civil Rights: Rhetoric or Reality* (New York: William Morrow and Company, 1984), pp. 15–16.

4. Greg Toppo, "Integrated Schools Still a Dream 50 Years Later," *USA Today* (April 28, 2004), pp. 1–2.

CHAPTER 6—A PERSONAL ODYSSEY

1. Paul R. Lawrence and Jay W. Lorsch, *Organization and Environment* (Boston: Harvard Business School Press, 1967). See also Jay W. Lorsch and Stephen A. Allen III, *Managing Diversity and Interdependence* (Boston: Harvard University Graduate School of Business Administration, Division of Research, 1973).

2. R. Roosevelt Thomas, Jr., "From Affirmative Action to Affirming Diversity," *Harvard Business Review* (March–April 1990), pp. 107–117.

3. R. Roosevelt Thomas, Jr., *Beyond Race and Gender: Unleashing the Power of Your Total Workforce by Managing Diversity* (New York: AMACOM, 1991), pp. 10–11.

4. R. Roosevelt Thomas, Jr., *Redefining Diversity* (New York: AMACOM, 1996), p. 5.

5. Ibid., p. 113.

6. R. Roosevelt Thomas, Jr., *Building a House for Diversity: How a Fable About a Giraffe & an Elephant Offers New Strategies for Today's Workforce* (New York: AMACOM, 1999), pp. 8–9.

CHAPTER 7—STRATEGIC DIVERSITY MANAGEMENT: UNDERGIRDING CONCEPTS

1. Nancy Wartik, "Hard-Wired for Prejudice? Experts Examine Human Response to Outsiders," *New York Times* Late Edition-Final (April 20, 2004), sec. F, p. 5.

2. Lawrence Blum, *"I'm Not a Racist, But . . ."* (Ithaca, NY: Cornell University Press, 2002), p. 15.

3. Ibid., p. 14.

4. Early versions of this discussion of Archie Bunker appeared in

the author's other writings: R. Roosevelt Thomas, Jr., "Lessons from Archie," *Profiles in Diversity Journal* (Summer 2001), pp. 16–17; and R. Roosevelt Thomas, Jr., "Building a Diversity Management Capability," in *The Portable MBA in Management,* 2nd ed., ed. Allan R. Cohen (New York: John Wiley & Sons, 2002) pp. 318–321.

CHAPTER 8—STRATEGIC DIVERSITY MANAGEMENT: FIVE FUNDAMENTALS

1. Cora Daniels, *Black Power Inc.: The New Voice of Success* (New York: John Wiley & Sons, 2004), p. 104.

SELECTED BIBLIOGRAPHY

American Academy of Arts & Sciences. *American Education: Still Separate Still Unequal.* Cambridge, MA: The American Academy of Arts & Sciences, 1995.

Baytos, Lawrence M. *Designing & Implementing Successful Diversity Programs.* Englewood Cliffs, NJ: Prentice Hall, 1995.

Bell, Derrick. *And We Are Not Saved—The Elusive Quest for Racial Justice.* New York: Basic Books, 1987.

Bell, Derrick. *Silent Covenants—Brown v. Board of Education and the Unfulfilled Hopes for Racial Reform.* New York: Oxford, 2004.

Blum, Lawrence. *"I'm Not a Racist, But . . .",* Ithaca, NY: Cornell University Press, 2002.

Blumrosen, Alfred W. and Blumrosen, Ruth G. *Slave Nation—How Slavery United the Colonies & Sparked the American Revolution.* Naperville, IL: Sourcebooks, 2005.

Brimelow, Peter. *Alien Nation: Common Sense About America's Immigration Disaster.* New York: Random House, 1995.

Buchanan, Patrick J. *The Death of the West.* New York: St. Martin's Press, 2002.

Burns, Stewart. *To the Mountaintop—Martin Luther King, Jr.'s Sacred Mission.* San Francisco: Harper, 2004.

Carson, Clayborne. *Civil Rights Chronicle.* Lincolnwood, IL: Legacy Publishing, 2003.

Carter, Stephen L. *Reflections of an Affirmative Action Baby.* New York: Basic Books, 1991.

Cashin, Sheryll. *The Failures of Integration—How Race and Class Are Undermining the American Dream.* New York: PublicAffairs, 2004.

Clotfelter, Charles T. *After Brown—The Rise and Retreat of School Desegregation.* Princeton, NJ: Princeton University Press, 2004.

Cobbs, Price M. and Turnock, Judith L. *Cracking the Corporate Code.* New York: AMACOM, 2003.

Connolly, Mickey and Rianoshek, Richard. *The Communication Catalyst: The Fast (But Not Stupid) Track to Value for Customers, Investors, and Employees.* Chicago: Dearborn Trade Publishing, 2002.

Cose, Ellis. *Beyond Brown v. Board: The Final Battle for Excellence in American Education.* New York: Rockefeller Foundation, 2004.

Cose, Ellis. *Bone to Pick—Of Forgiveness, Reconciliation, Reparation and Revenge.* New York: Atria Books, 2004.

Cose, Ellis. *Color-Blind: Seeing Beyond Race in a Race-Obsessed World.* New York: HarperCollins Publishers, 1997.

Cose, Ellis. *The Rage of a Privileged Class—Why Are Middle-Class Blacks Angry? Why Should America Care?* New York: HarperCollins Publishers, 1993.

Cox, Taylor. *Cultural Diversity in Organizations.* San Francisco: Berrett-Hoehler, 1993.

Cruse, Harold. *Plural but Equal—Blacks and Minorities in America's Plural Society.* New York: William Morrow and Company, 1987.

Daniels, Cora. *Black Power Inc.: The New Voice of Success.* New York: Wiley, 2004.

Dickerson, Debra J. *The End of Blackness.* New York: Pantheon Books, 2004.

D'Souza, Dinesh. *The End of Racism.* New York: The Free Press, 1995.

Dudziak, Mary L. *Cold War Civil Rights: Race and the Image of American Democracy.* Princeton, NJ: Princeton University Press, 2000.

Dyson, Michael Eric. *I May Not Get There with You: The True Story of Martin Luther King, Jr.* New York: The Free Press, 2000.

Eastland, Terry. *Ending Affirmative Action—The Case for Colorblind Justice.* New York: Basic Books, 1996.

Edley, Christopher, Jr. *Not All Black and White—Affirmative Action and American Values.* New York: Hill and Wang, 1996.

Ellis, Joseph J. *Founding Brothers—The Revolutionary Generation.* New York: Alfred A. Knopf, 2001.

Fluker, Walter E. *They Looked for a City: A Comparative Analysis of Community in the Thought of Howard Thurman and Martin Luther King, Jr.* Lanham, MD: University Press of America, 1989.

Frady, Marshall. *Martin Luther King, Jr.* New York: Viking Penguin, 2002.

Frankel, Max. "Reaffirm the Affirmative," *New York Times* magazine, February 26, 1995.

Frazier, E. Franklin. *The Negro in the United States.* Toronto, Ontario: The Macmillan Company, 1949.

Gardner, John W. *Excellence.* New York: W. W. Norton & Company, 1984.

Gardner, John W. *Living, Leading, and the American Dream.* San Francisco: Jossey-Bass, 2003.

Garrow, David J. *Bearing the Cross.* New York: William Morrow and Company, 1986.

Glazer, Nathan. *Affirmative Discrimination: Ethnic Inequality and Public Policy.* New York: Basic Books, 1975.

Glazer, Nathan. *We Are All Multiculturalists Now.* Cambridge, MA: Harvard University Press, 1997.

Glazer, Nathan and Moynihan, Daniel P. *Beyond the Melting Pot—The Negroes, Puerto Ricans, Jews, Italians, and Irish of New York City.* Cambridge, MA: The MIT Press, 2001.

Greenberg, Stanley B. *The Two Americas—Our Current Political Deadlock and How to Break It.* New York: St. Martin's Press, 2004.

Grier, William H. and Cobbs, Price M. *Black Rage.* New York: Basic Books, 1968.

Griggs, Lewis Brown and Louw, Lente-Louise. *Valuing Diversity: New Tools for a New Reality.* New York: McGraw-Hill, 1995.

Himmelfarb, Gertrude. *One Nation, Two Cultures.* New York: Alfred A. Knopf, 1999.

Hollinger, David A. *Postethnic America.* New York: Basic Books, 1995.

Huntington, Samuel P. *Who Are We? The Challenge to America's National Identity.* New York: Simon & Schuster, 2004.

Iwata, Kay. *The Power of Diversity—5 Essential Competencies for Leading a Diverse Workforce.* Petaluma, CA: Global Insights Publishing, 2004.

Jacoby, Tamar. *Someone Else's House: America's Unfinished Struggle for Integration.* New York: The Free Press, 1998.

King, Martin Luther, Jr. "The Ethical Demands for Integration," in *A Testament of Hope: The Essential Writings of Martin Luther King, Jr.,* ed. James M. Washington. San Francisco: Harper & Row, 1986.

King, Martin Luther, Jr. *Where Do We Go from Here: Chaos or Community?* Boston: Beacon, 1967.

Klarman, Michael. *From Jim Crow to Civil Rights: The Supreme Court and the Struggle for Racial Equality.* New York: Oxford University Press, 2004.

Klinkner, Philip A. *The Unsteady March.* Chicago: The University of Chicago Press, 1999.

Lasch-Quinn, Elisabeth. *Race Experts.* New York: W. W. Norton & Company, 2001.

Lawrence, Paul R. and Lorsch, Jay W. *Organization and Environment.* Boston: Harvard Business School Press, 1967.

Lewis, David L. *King—A Biography.* Urbana: University of Illinois Press, 1978.

Lorsch, Jay W. and Allen, Stephen A, III. *Managing Diversity and Interdependence—An Organizational Study of Multidivisional Firms.* Boston: Harvard University, 1973.

Loury, Glenn C. *The Anatomy of Racial Inequality.* Cambridge, MA: Harvard University Press, 2002.

Loury, Glenn C. *One by One from the Inside Out—Essays and Reviews on Race and Responsibility in America.* New York: The Free Press, 1995.

Lynch, Frederick R. *The Diversity Machine.* New York: The Free Press, 1997.

Lynch, Frederick R. *Invisible Victims—White Males and the Crisis of Affirmative Action.* New York: Greenwood, 1989.

Marable, Manning. *The Great Wells of Democracy—The Meaning of Race in American Life*. New York, BasicCivitas Books, 2002.

McGovern, George. *The Essential America—Our Founders and the Liberal Tradition*. New York: Simon & Schuster, 2004.

McMahon, Kevin. *Reconsidering Roosevelt on Race: How the Presidency Paved the Road to Brown*. Chicago: The University of Chicago Press, 2004.

Morris, Aldon D. *The Origins of the Civil Rights Movement*. New York: The Free Press, 1984.

Morrison, Ann M. *The New Leaders—Guidelines on Leadership Diversity in America*. San Francisco: Jossey-Bass, 1992.

Myrdal, Gunnar. *An American Dilemma—The Negro Problem and Modern Democracy*. New York: Harper & Row, 1944.

National Urban League. "Diversity Practices That Work: The American Worker Speaks," survey report. New York: National Urban League, 2004.

Oates, Stephen B. *Let the Trumpet Sound—The Life of Martin Luther King, Jr*. New York: Harper & Row, 1982.

Ogletree, Charles. *All Deliberate Speed: Reflections on the First Half-Century of Brown v. Board of Education*. New York: W. W. Norton & Company, 2004.

Patterson, James T. *Brown v. Board of Education—A Civil Rights Milestone and Its Troubled Legacy*. New York: Oxford University Press, 2001.

Patterson, Orlando. *The Ordeal of Integration—Progress and Resentment in America's "Racial" Crisis*. Washington, DC: Civitas, 1997.

Puddington, Arch. "What to Do About Affirmative Action," *Commentary*, June 1995, pp. 21–28.

Roberts, Paul Craig and Stratton, Lawrence M. "Color Code," *National Review*, March 20, 1995, pp. 36–51, 80.

Rosen, Jeffrey. "The Color Blind Court," *The New Republic*, July 31, 1995, pp. 19–25.

Schlesinger, Arthur M., Jr. *The Disuniting of America*. New York: W. W. Norton & Company, 1992.

Schwarz, Benjamin. "The Diversity Myth: America's Leading Export," *Atlantic Monthly*, May 1995.

Shipler, David K. *A Country of Strangers—Blacks and Whites in America*. New York: Alfred A. Knopf, 1997.

Silberman, Charles E. *Crisis in Black and White*. New York: Random House, 1964.

Sleeper, Jim. *Liberal Racism*. New York: Penguin Group, 1997.

Sowell, Thomas. *Civil Rights: Rhetoric or Reality*. New York: William Morrow and Company, 1984.

Steel, Shelby. *The Content of Our Character*. New York: St. Martin's Press, 1990.

Steel, Shelby. *A Dream Deferred—The Second Betrayal of Black Freedom in America*. New York: HarperCollins, 1998.

Steinberg, Stephen. *Turning Back: The Retreat from Racial Justice in American Thought and Policy*. Boston: Beacon, 1995.

Sunnemark, Fredrik. *Ring Out Freedom! The Voice of Martin Luther King, Jr. and the Making of the Civil Rights Movement*. Bloomington: Indiana University Press, 2004.

Taylor, Jared. *Paved with Good Intentions*. New York: Carroll & Graf Publishers, 1992.

Thernstrom, Stephan, and Abigail Thernstrom. *America in Black and White—One Nation, Indivisible*. New York: Simon & Schuster, 1997.

Thernstrom, Stephan, and Abigail Thernstrom. *No Excuses—Closing the Racial Gap in Learning*. New York: Simon & Schuster, 2003.

Thomas, Bettye Collier and Franklin, V. P. *My Soul Is a Witness—A Chronology of the Civil Rights Era, 1954–1965*. New York: Henry Holt and Company, 1999.

Thomas, David A. and Gabarro, John J. *Breaking Through—The Making of Minority Executives in Corporate America*. Boston: Harvard Business School Press, 1999.

Thomas, R. Roosevelt, Jr. *Beyond Race and Gender: Unleashing the Power of Your Total Workforce by Managing Diversity*. New York: AMACOM, 1991.

Thomas, R. Roosevelt, Jr. "Building a Diversity Management Capability," in *The Portable MBA in Management* (2nd ed.), ed. Allan R. Cohen. New York: Wiley, 2002.

Thomas, R. Roosevelt, Jr. *Building a House for Diversity: How a Fable*

About a Giraffe & an Elephant Offers New Strategies for Today's Workforce. New York: AMACOM, 1999.

Thomas, R. Roosevelt, Jr. "From Affirmative Action to Affirming Diversity," *Harvard Business Review*, March–April 1990.

Thomas, R. Roosevelt, Jr. "Lessons from Archie Bunker," *Profiles in Diversity Journal*, Summer 2001.

Thomas, R. Roosevelt, Jr. *Redefining Diversity.* New York: AMACOM, 1996.

Thurman, Howard. *The Search for Common Ground.* Richmond, IN: Friends United Press, 1971.

Toppo, Greg. "Integrated Schools Still a Dream 50 Years Later," *USA Today*, April 28, 2004.

Ture, Kwame and Hamilton, Charles V. *Black Power—The Politics of Liberation.* New York: Random House, 1992.

Wartik, Nancy. "Hard-Wired for Prejudice? Experts Examine Human Response to Outsiders," *New York Times*, April 20, 2004, sec. F, p. 5.

West, Cornel. *Democracy Matters.* New York: The Penguin Press, 2004.

West, Cornel. *Race Matters.* Boston: Beacon, 1993.

Wicker, Tom. *Tragic Failure—Racial Integration in America.* New York: William Morrow and Company, 1996.

Wilkins, Roger. "Racism Has Its Privileges: The Case for Affirmative Action," *The Nation*, March 27, 1995, pp. 409–416.

Winbush, Raymond A., ed. *Should America Pay? Slavery and the Raging Debate on Reparations.* New York: Amistad (an imprint of HarperCollins Publishing), 2003.

Wolfe, Alan. *One Nation After All.* New York: Penguin Group, 1998.

Wooten, Jim. "Our Opinion: Democratic Coup Under Gold Dome," *The Atlanta Journal-Constitution*, September 2, 2001, p. D-8.

INDEX

acculturation, in Strategic Diversity Management (SDM), 157, 158, 159
adaptation, in Strategic Diversity Management (SDM), 157–158, 159
affirmative action, 49–63
  case against, 57–59
  case for, 53–57
  diversity as euphemism for, 7, 123
  diversity management capability and, 56–57, 61–63, 87, 123
  future of, 59–61
  independence of, 10
  life expectancy of, 50–51
  origins of, 51–53
  "outreach," 51–53
  present status of, 59
  Supreme Court decisions concerning, 49–50, 59
All in the Family (TV series), 108–115
alternative frameworks
  importance of embracing, 81
  recognizing, 154
American creed
  Beloved Community and, 42–43
  contradictions in, 38–39
  nature of, 26–29, 41, 43
American Dilemma, An (Myrdal), 38–39
American Experiment (Schlesinger)
  conditions for success of, 31
  current state of, 24–28
  experiment, defined, 22
  future of, 28–30
  historical overview of, 22–24
  lack of awareness of, 27–28
  multicultural alternative to, 30
  as multiethnic society, 21–22
  refusal to be discouraged, 32
  as will of the land, 31
American Institute for Managing Diversity (AIMD)
  evolution of concept of diversity, 93
  founding of, 86, 87
Anglo-Protestant culture, 29

225

ABOUT THE AUTHOR

FOR MORE THAN 20 YEARS, Dr. R. Roosevelt Thomas, Jr., has been at the forefront of developing and implementing innovative concepts and strategies for maximizing organizational and individual potential through diversity management. He currently serves as the president and CEO of Roosevelt Thomas Consulting & Training, Inc., and president of The American Institute for Managing Diversity (AIMD).

In 1984, concerned about the inability of America's organizations to maximize the contribution of diverse employees, Dr. Thomas founded AIMD as a nonprofit research and education enterprise. He and his staff became known as the seminal source for diversity management concepts and strategies. The team focused initially on workforce diversity. They later expanded their focus to create a diversity framework for addressing general management issues such as change management, functional coordination, the integration of multiple lines of business, and acquisitions and mergers.

Dr. Thomas is the author of four published books: *Building a House for Diversity: A Fable About a Giraffe & an Elephant Offers New Strategies for Today's Workforce*; *Redefining Diversity*; *Differences Do Make a Difference*; and *Beyond Race and Gender: Unleashing the Power of Your Total Work Force by Managing Diversity*. He is also the author of numerous articles, such as the *Harvard Business Review* article "From Affirmative Action to Affirming Diversity," which alerted Corporate America to the need for moving beyond EEO in addressing the challenge of empowering a diverse workforce.

Dr. Thomas earned a D.B.A. in Organizational Behavior from Harvard University, an M.B.A. in Finance from the University of Chicago, and a B.A. in Mathematics *Summa Cum Laude* from Morehouse College, where he was elected to Phi Beta Kappa. He has also served as Secretary of Morehouse College, Dean of the Graduate School of Business Administration at Atlanta University, assistant professor at the Harvard Business School, and instructor at Morehouse College.

In 1998, the National Academy of Human Resources elected and installed Dr. Thomas as a Fellow. He has also been recognized by The *Wall Street Journal* as one of the top ten consultants in the country, and cited by *Human Resource Executive* as one of HR's Most Influential People. In 1995, he received the American Society for Training and Development's "Distinguished Contribution to Human Resource Development" Award. Dr. Thomas joined the Society for Human Resource Management's Board of Directors in 2003.